When Hearts
Were Brave Again
and Arms Were Strong

When Hearts Were Brave Again

and Arms Were Strong

A Limited Service Soldier's
Great Adventure
1943-1945

Philip A. Langehough, Pfc
304th Combat Engineers Battalion Co A
79th Infantry Division

AUGUST 2004

When Hearts Were Brave Again
and Arms Were Strong

Publisher: Information International
Copyright 2005, Philip A. Langehough
Printed in Canada

Library of Congress Cataloging-in-Publication Data

Langehough, Philip A., 1924-
    When hearts were brave again and arms were strong : a limited service
    soldier's great adventure, 1943-1945 / by Philip A. Langehough.
    p. cm.
    Library of Congress Control Number: 2005926250
    ISBN 1-882480-12-0
1. Langehough, Philip A., 1924- 2. United States. Army Engineer Combat
Battalion, 304th. 3. World War, 1939-1945—Campaigns—Western Front.
4. World War, 1939-1945—Campaigns—France. 5. World War,
1939-1945—Personal narratives, American. 6. Military engineers—United
    States—Biography. I. Title.
D769.335304th .L36 2005   940.54'1273'092—dc22

                                             2004029430

DEDICATION

"Time like an ever rolling stream
soon bears all its sons away
They lie forgotten as a dream
dies at the opening day." *

This book is dedicated to the men of the 304th Combat Engineers Battalion and the 79th Infantry Division.

I hope it will help to keep alive the memory of their gallant service so that it will not fade from the collective memory of the American people.

The title of this work, "When Hearts Were Brave Again and Arms Were Strong," is from verse 5 of "For All The Saints."**

* Verse 5, "O God Our Help in Ages Past," Isaac Watt
** Verse 6, "For All the Saints," William W. How

FOREWORD

This project has been in the back, or front, of my mind for a long time. I have several reasons for taking the enormous amount of time and effort to write it: Primarily, I wanted to tell my own story of my great adventure in the Army. Secondly, and more importantly, I wanted to tell the larger story of the men with whom I shared battle, the men of the 304th Combat Engineers Battalion and the 79th Infantry Division. I wanted to tell each of these stories in my own way, integrating my own experiences with my extensive reading and research into combat operations of these units during World War II.

I wish to thank my late wife of many years, Emily Langehough, for providing both the lifelong and daily inspiration to me to get this project started and off the ground. I would like to thank my wonderful friends, family and supporters, especially my Christian family at Luther Place and the Prince William Senior Center for their support and guidance.

Finally, I would like to thank my friends Paula Ernst and Dave Warner for all their assistance in turning my research and work into something better than what I ever hoped it could be, and for helping me to realize my dream of preserving my memories of my service in the Army during World War II. Great job guys!

I hope that you enjoy reading about my stories and memories—it truly was an amazing, thrilling, frightening, wonderfully awful and awfully wonderful time of my life.

—Phil A. Langehough
August, 2004

CONTENTS

In the Army Now 1

Fort Leonard Wood 6

Camp Laguna, Arizona 17

Camp Phillips, Kansas 22

The Explorer 29

England 34

Normandy Landing 46

Normandy – Hedgerows 64

Normandy Breakout 75

The Seine River to Belgium 88

Third Army XV Corps / Seventh Army 99

The Seventh Army 105

Vosges to Alsace 118

Battle for Alsace-Nordwind 129

To the Rhine River 151

The End of the Fighting 155

Sudetenland 166

Life in the Army.. 188

Mines, Bridges, Roads
   The Keynote of the Combat Engineers 217

Men of Company A 304th
   Combat Engineers Battalion.......................... 220

Eight Men of the 79th Division
circa 194

Second Squad, Second Platoon
Front Row: Garcia, Floyd, Zilliot, Ostepac
Second Row: Mulato, Fafel, Barnes, Walters, Carr, Thell, Romero

Marvin C. Sartorius shows us his
"Camp Laguna Smile"
October, 1943

Second Platoon NCOs (Non-Commissioned Officers)
Front Row: Sartorius, McIntosh, Lindsey
Second Row: McQuary, Langston, Ward

My family, 1943

Philip A. Langehough, Lyle, Minn.

NOTICE TO REGISTRANT
TO APPEAR FOR
PHYSICAL EXAMINATION

(STAMP OF LOCAL BOARD)

12-23-42
(Date)

You are hereby directed to report to _____ Dr. Melzer _____
(Name of examining physician)

at _____ Lyle, Minn. _____ for physical examination at 3 p___ m.,
(Address)

on _____ Dec. 28, 1942 _____ Failure to do so may result in your
being declared a delinquent and subjected to the penalties provided by law.

Chief Clerk
D. S. S. Form No. 201 _____ Member of Local Board.
(Revised 6-1-41)   16—18635

Physical Examination Notice, 1942

1

In The Army Now

This story begins in the men's dormitory at St. Olaf College, Northfield, Minnesota in 1943, crosses the World War II battlefields of Europe, and ends with an honorable discharge from Camp McCoy, Wisconsin in 1945.

Each and every day of those thirty months, I considered it an honor to serve in the largest and best army that the United States of America has ever produced. At nineteen years of age, I entered the army an insecure young man. Thirty months later I emerged as a confident twenty-one year-old able to handle anything the world tossed my way.

The US Army inherited by George Marshall in 1939 was a threat to no one; it ranked 19th in the world with a total of 174,000 men. Its few divisions were mostly at half strength, and scattered worldwide in posts offering little opportunity to train as full units. Maneuvers were held every four years.

The miracle was that, by August of 1943, as described by David Kennedy in "Freedom from Fear":

> *"Young men had begun pouring into the Selective Service centers for physical and psychological examinations in the last week of 1940. Eventually nearly eighteen million were examined and they were a remarkable composite portrait of a generation's physical and mental makeup. Most were judged*

fit for service, though two million were rejected for neurological or psychological reasons, and four million more for medical and educational deficiencies...to meet its manpower needs, the Army eventually undertook remedial work for the draftees. Some twenty-five thousand dentists pulled fifteen million teeth, and fitted 2.5 million sets of dentures. Army optometrists fitted 2.25 million pairs of glasses, and special Army schools bestowed the gift of literacy on almost a million recruits.

"The average GI was nearly twenty-six years old in 1944...he stood five feet eight inches and weighed 144 pounds. Four out of ten white but fewer than two out of ten black draftees had finished high school. Almost a third of whites and more than half of black recruits had no education beyond grade school. The statistical average GI had completed one year of high school."[1]

Those of us who survived the war laid up a store of memories that time could not corrode—indeed memories embroidered by times in indulgent hand. Benjamin Bradley, former editor of the Washington Post, spoke for many veterans when he remembered the war as "...more exciting, more meaningful than anything I'd ever done. This is why I had such a wonderful time in the war, I just plain loved it. I loved the excitement, the sense of achievement, the camaraderie and even loved being a little bit scared, The responsibility and anticipation are overpowering. The ignorance is instructive. The fear of disgrace is consuming; and survival is triumphant"[2]

Ben Bradley's words rang true in my heart when he said, "I can't say I enjoyed every minute, but at the same time, every day taught lessons in how to survive and have a great adventure at the same time."

---

[1] Kennedy 710
[2] Kennedy 712 – 713

War could not only be exciting, it also provided "an escape from the every day into a special world where the bonds that hold us to our duties in daily life—the bonds of family, community, work—disappear. In war, all bets are off. It's the frontier beyond the last settlement. It's Las Vegas."

The soldiers' wartime behavior was much more lax than considered acceptable in society, and many men reveled in it. The "eat, drink and be merry" philosophy not only helped the GI forget the horrors of combat, but it was also fun. Veterans usually denounced combat's horrors and hardships, yet they would not deny that their wartime experiences were exciting, adventuresome, and a great sense of pride. Most of the soldiers remember the good times and their close relationship with their squad and platoon-mates."[3]

In December of 1942, times were unsettled in the men's dormitory. Every day brought one less student in college and one more student drafted. We speculated whether or not we would survive the war, whether or not we would return to St. Olaf College. In January 1943, the Navy took over the dormitory for V12 students. All of us were displaced and my new roommate, Merlin Davey, and I finished the school year in a room off campus. Each one of my friends survived the war and most graduated with me in the Class of 1948.

On the second day of that Christmas vacation, I reported to old Dr. Melzer for my pre-induction physical. He had trouble finding a vein, leaving both arms scarred, until he finally drew some blood. Six brief months later, on June 19th, my father drove me to Austin, Minnesota, to join forty young men for a bus ride to Fort Snelling, Minneapolis.

---

[3] Kindsvatter 180 – 185

During our physical, we disrobed and carried our clothing from one doctor to the next. At the conclusion of the physical, two doctors told me I was exempt from service due to one bad eye and high blood pressure. I insisted there must be someplace I could serve my country. After further discussion, they relented by assigning me to limited service with instructions to report on June 30th, 1943. As it turned out, I never served a day of limited service in the thirty months of duty, nor did I want any consideration as a limited service soldier.

I reported for duty on June 30 to the Army Reception Center at Fort Snelling, Minneapolis. We bunked in new barracks. The first few days were spent with tests to determine intelligence and aptitude. I took my time answering the test questions, concentrating on the math and science parts. Our indoctrination sessions took a day or two. Then we reported for duty after breakfast. Sawing large logs with a crosscut saw was the main job assigned. My partner and I did just enough sawing to not attract attention. They must have had trouble placing me since I remained at Fort Snelling for five weeks.

Kitchen Patrol (KP) was expected on a regular basis. It was very hard work to serve two meals one hour apart, one at noon and the other at 1:00 p.m. In only a single hour, KPs had to wash dishes, pots and pans and reset the tables. On the fourth of July, not many men showed up for meals so each of the KPs got a large bowl of Jell-O fruit salad to eat. I wasn't able to face a bowl of Jell-O fruit salad for a long time.

Nights and weekends were spent watching movies at the post theater. The first movie I saw was an all-black cast of "Stormy Weather." Many nights we rode the trolley to downtown Minneapolis or St. Paul to feast on ice cream at Bridgeman's. I spent several Saturdays visiting my Aunt Marie and Uncle Carl. We enjoyed picnics at some of the many lakes.

Finally, the day came to board the train for Fort Leonard Wood, Missouri, and thirteen weeks of Combat Engineers Basic Training. There must have been 200 to 300 recruits from Fort Snelling. We rode World War I vintage day coaches. The pace was slow because we were sidetracked frequently to allow freight and passenger trains to pass by. About four o'clock in the afternoon, we pulled into St. Louis and performed 30 minutes of close order drill, even though the thermometer registered 104 degrees. Wringing wet, we got back on the train and sat near open windows to cool off, in spite of the ashes and soot raining in from outside.

We noticed the hills and the Ozark Mountains and came into Leonard Wood about 1:30 a.m. We got off the train and enjoyed doughnuts and coffee, served by the unwilling and unfortunate KPs that had to work at that hour. We arrived at the new barracks at 2:30 a.m., selected a bunk, undressed and were asleep by 3:30 a.m. (Historically, troop trains arrived at their destination after midnight). At 6:30 a.m., we were awakened for our first day of training. A trainload of GI's from Maryland, Virginia and Pennsylvania arrived the same day. I attended a funeral in June 2001 to read in his obituary that the deceased worked building the barracks in 1941 prior to his induction.

2

Fort Leonard Wood

To improve the poor basic training experienced in WWI, General Marshall was convinced that men performed better and were less likely to protest if they understood why they were serving and what they were contributing to the national defense. He directed the army commanders to explain what they were defending and why it was necessary that they do their part. [4]

General Marshall believed that the greatest problem of wartime was to offer training that lasted long enough. "If it is

[4] Pogue Ordeal & Hope 117 – 118

not well done and thoroughly done, the troops are going to be lacking in discipline. I had some professional facts gathered go around for me. They saw the men in training in this country and asked them what they thought of it—(later) they found the same men in the front after they had been engaged in action) and (nearly everything) the men objected to, they now said they had not had enough of."[5]

Missouri's Fort Leonard Wood is a center for US Army engineer training. It covers 90,000 acres and lies in the Mark Twain Forest, 130 miles southwest of St. Louis. The post was built in 1941 and named for Major General Leonard E. Wood, Army Chief of Staff from 1910 to 1914. During World War II, 320,000 men were trained at the Engineers Training Center. An infantry division also trained there. The Corps of Engineers is headquartered there as well as the Chief Training Center. Fort Leonard Wood had a bad reputation, since it was miles from civilization in the Ozark Mountains. One small town nearby was referred to as Gonorrhea Gulch at Rolla.

Upon reflection, I found Fort Leonard Wood offered the best in facilities, especially its barracks, post exchange, and theaters. The prices at the PX were very low; the soda fountain featured nine-cent sundaes. A new juke box featured pictures of the performing groups—a forerunner of television. Four songs I remember were *"Deep In The Heart of Texas," "Pistol Packing Mama," "To Hear the Chime Bells Ring,"* and the *"Boogie Woogie Bugle Boy of Company B."* There was an area of tables lighted at night, and since they served beer at the PX, getting a table was always a problem. The barbershop gave us short haircuts. Rookies were intimidated by the barbers and succumbed to "the works" for $5.00—a big chunk of the $50.00 we were paid. Trainees were exempt from KP at Fort Leonard

---

[5] Pogue – George Marshall – Interview, February 1, 1957

Wood. Instead, German prisoners from Rommel's Afrika Korps performed service tasks in the kitchen and laundry. The men from the Afrika Korps were prime physical specimens, described by William L. Shirer as "The German soldiers were tanned, clean-cut, robust, their bodies fully developed, their teeth white, healthy looking as lions."[6] In all, there were some 400,000 German serving in prison camps throughout the US.

The first day was spent getting to know the thirty-five men in our platoon and the 170 men in Company A that I was assigned to. The staff consisted of Captain Long, Sergeant Vaughn and Corporal Frisby. Platoon and squad leaders were selected from the enlisted ranks, generally men with some ROTC training. Our platoon leader was a graduate of Texas A & M. Captain Long, an older gray-haired man, directed and handled recruits extremely well. One of the lieutenants, a red-haired graduate of the University of Texas, was a born leader of men. Sgt. Vaughan, an old army type in his early forties, treated us with respect in a firm but fair manner. Corporal Frisby, a Mormon from Utah, was full of enthusiasm and always encouraged us to finish the job and do it right.

Fresh from civilian life, the men suddenly found themselves part of a strange and different world. In a matter of days, they were run through a gigantic treadmill of army induction—a treadmill designed to transform a man from a civilian to a soldier. The men in the squad were assigned by height; being 5' 7½", I was next to the last man.[7]

After the reception process, recruits were broken into platoons of about forty for the duration of the training. As part of the platoon, the recruit continued the process started at the reception center by learning to make his bunk, maintain

---

[6] Shirer 515
[7] History of the 313th, 20

his footlocker, and keep his uniform and equipment to the demanding standards of the drill sergeant. Almost every minute of his day was regulated. Uniformity was required. The recruits learned to march, talk and look the same. One recruit realized it was a 'process of surrender' of individual personality and freedom. In order to meet group standards of appearance and behavior; at every turn, at every hour, it seemed, a habit or preference had to be given up, an adjustment had to made. "Many recruits found...this loss of individuality alarming and demeaning: You quickly lost your identity in the sense that you became a number very quickly, or an item" [8]

The first week was basic training orientation. We saw films of every aspect: training, rifle, military courtesy. To implement George Marshall's idea that men fought better and were less likely to protest when they understood why they were serving and what they were contributing to the national defense, we were shown a series of films by Frank Capra entitled *Why We Fight*. Each episode was intended to motivate every soldier to do his part. The post theater was a large air-conditioned building with regular theater seats. At the conclusion of the *Why We Fight* films, officers selected five or six to lead small group discussion sessions. I was selected to be a discussion group leader. However, the discussion wasn't very lively, since most soldiers were not interested in the topic.

The breaking of our civilian spirit started almost immediately. We were issued two pairs of shoes: one pair was laced with an X the other laced with an =. We were required to wear shoes with an X Monday, Wednesday, and Friday and shoes with an = on Tuesday, Thursday and Saturday. This system prevented soldiers from saving one

---

[8] Leckie 10

pair for inspection. If one was caught wearing the wrong laces, he was given extra duty.

We went to bed at 3:30 a.m. the first night, and were aroused at 7:00 a.m. for a full day of duty. Friday evening or Saturday morning was spent in cleaning the barracks floor and latrine. On Saturday morning each soldier's bed was made with snowcaps and his equipment laid out. Our barracks was gigged at every inspection, which meant we had to clean the barracks on Saturday and Sunday. This gigging was done to defeat our civilian spirit.

On a night compass reading exercise, we got back to the barracks at 3:30 a.m. and were roused again at 7:00 a.m. for a full day of duty. Every drill and exercise was to impress each recruit that it was the army way or nothing. A common saying was that "The army can't make you do anything, but they could make you wish you had."

A typical training day:

> 6:05 a.m. Reveille
>
> 7:00 a.m. Breakfast
>
> 7:30 a.m. Clean barracks and
> police area
>
> 8:00 a.m. - 12:00 Noon Training
>
> 12:00 p.m. Lunch
>
> 1:00-5:30 p.m. Training
>
> 6:00-7:00 p.m. Dinner
>
> 9:45 p.m. Lights Out

I saw the purposes of basic training as:

1. Physical conditioning so men could stand the rigors of combat conditions.

2. Acquiring military and discipline skills, as well as specific skills of the branch, whether infantry, or combat engineers, etc.

3. Breaking the civilian spirit to replace it with military spirit so that men could follow orders.

Each day of the thirteen weeks was programmed to produce completely trained combat engineers by the end. The first week's training concentrated on close order drills and rifle training. Instructional film, followed by intense hands-on rifle work, enabled us to eventually assemble our rifles blindfolded.

Next we concentrated on mastering several firing positions: prone, kneeling and standing. Finally, the day came to go to the rifle firing range. There must have been fifty or more firing stations. We qualified on the 200 – 300 and 500 yards ranges. We fired both slow and rapid fire. After firing eight rounds, the men working in the pits would pull and mark the target. Then we had rapid-fire exercise that involved firing twenty-six shots in thirty seconds.

Since I have almost no vision in my right eye, I fired with my left hand in the rapid fire. I had to put the rifle down to reload and I fired on the next target. I shot sharpshooter, the next target shot expert. When not firing, we took turns in the pits. Using a flag and a target machine system, each shooter was informed of his score. It was interesting but tiring work. Dropping a rifle was an almost unforgivable sin. The recruit that dropped his rifle had to carry it with him for two days, even taking it to bed with him. One of the last requirements was to crawl under barbed wire for 100 yards with machine guns firing over the men at forty inches off the ground.

Trainees Building Bridges
Fort Leonard Wood
(I'm in this picture somewhere!)

Completed Wooden Bridge
Fort Leonard Wood

TYPES OF TRAINING

1. Chemical Warfare

We entered an area full of tear gas. We were told that when we smelled the gas, to put on our gas masks. Since many had difficulty adjusting their masks, they got an unpleasantly large whiff of the tear gas.

2. Obstacle Course

The obstacle course was a fixture in every basic training program. Its aim was to train the GI to move forward quickly and without mishap, despite obstacles in his path.

The course consisted of walls of varying heights, a lattice work of logs, over which we had to run, a pond to jump across, then a pond we swung over on a rope, a sewer pipe to crawl through, and last, a fifteen foot wall to scale to the top and then jump down to the ground.

3. Engineer Training

We trained in all the tools of the trade: from picks and shovels to jack hammers. We built all manner of bridges: the Bailey bridge, pontoon bridges, footbridges, etc. (See pictures). We practiced exiting a simulated landing craft that was moving up and down to mimic ocean waves. Each soldier had to swim the length of an olympic-sized swimming pool. One soldier who said he couldn't swim was told to crawl along the bottom. Men who failed the test were required to take swimming lessons.

4. Physical Training

We had rifle exercises each day. Hikes of 5, 10, 15 and 26 miles were scheduled. At the start I did not think I had any chance of walking 26 miles. In fact, it was much more as we carried field packs and rifles. I sucked hard candy, which helped me carry on one step at a time until the hike was over. The steep inclines added to the effort required, especially Separation Hill—so-called because it separated the men from the boys. I was the next to last walker in the platoon and received strength from Sgt. Vaughn, who held down the rear. I have suffered from hypertension since age sixteen. In fact, during the last two years of high school, I had to take a nap every afternoon, so basic training was a big physical challenge for me. I told myself that if a forty year-old could make each march, I could do it too. At the completion of the twenty-six mile hike, when we took off the heavy pack, we were almost light headed and found it hard to walk a straight line without staggering. Several men fell out, and a couple rode home on the ambulance.

Training was conducted in an orderly manner, with every exercise done in a professional way. The officers and NCOs handled the men in a strict but fair manner—and there was no hazing or abuse. The army of 1943 had no place for today's marine drill instructor. The basic instructional technique employed was the same regardless of the skill being taught: demonstration, explanation, and performance. During thirteen weeks of basic training, I talked to most of my platoon mates and discovered that the majority had never traveled more than 100 miles from home. In fact, very few men had even visited another state.

During the tearing-down process, the recruit could not see what any of this training had to do with preparing him for combat. Learning to shine shoes, march, salute, pull kitchen duty, and make a bunk in snowcaps did not strike him as useful skills. After two to three weeks of training, the recruits hit an absolute low point. Just when recruits were almost at the bottom, things began to change. The teardown part ended and the buildup phase began and they were rebuilt as soldiers. This phase began by teaching military skills beginning with the rifle, hand grenades, bayonets, and marches of varying length to build up stamina.

There were several men older than forty in my squad. One was in good shape and had no problems with the strenuous training. One soldier from Baltimore had trouble getting used to army life. He argued and complained about almost everything. Once he fell as asleep in the barber's chair, and the barber, egged on by the waiting men, shaved the poor man's head. The next day a dentist pulled his teeth. His bald head and the toothless mouth were more than he could stand. He sobbed and cried so much that he was given a medical discharge. By the end of basic training, a real transformation had taken place. An angry demoralized private had become a physically fit, mentally tough, self-confident soldier. We started the basic training with the attitude we couldn't walk twenty-five miles or work all night and then be required to work the following day. After thirteen weeks of training together the platoon had become a genuine unit bound by hundreds of common experiences. We had completed two of the goals—we were in combat-ready physical condition, and we trained in most areas facing combat engineers. At the end of the training, we had been indoctrinated to work together as part of a military team. We had also become friends.[9]

Three-day passes were issued on the last day of training. I joined two Jewish men and went to Springfield, Missouri. We stayed at the YMCA and went sight seeing without incident. However, on Saturday evening, we went into an

---

9 Kindsvatter 24

eating-place. A waiter called them Christ killers and kicked us out. This was the first anti-Semitism I had ever experienced, since Minnesota is very accepting in racial matters.* I apologized for the racist man and said I accepted every one as equals.

The day came when most of the men shipped out were in units awaiting an overseas call. After a couple of days, four of us got word we were joining the 304th Combat Engineers, 79th Infantry Division at Camp Laguna, Arizona. We boarded the train and two days later arrived at Yuma, Arizona.

* The men of E Company in *"Band of Brothers"* had the same and worse experiences.

3

79th Infantry Division
Camp Laguna, Arizona

We were dumped off the train at a siding in the desert near Yuma, with nothing in sight except tumble weeds and trash blowing in the strong wind. No one came to meet us. We later learned that the 79th Infantry Division had instructed the army that no more replacements were to be sent as they were moving to Camp Phillips, Kansas, in early December 1943. Apparently, our journey from Missouri to Kansas was to be by way of Arizona.

The three of us suggested to the man in charge that we look around the city before calling the 304th Combat Engineers. He called the 304th Combat Engineers and, within an hour, they sent a truck to pick us up. We were dumped off in a tent city surrounded by desert scenery—nothing but sand and cactus.

We were led to Captain Varnum's tent where one of our party forgot to salute, which resulted in a lecture on military courtesy—a bad start to the new life in an infantry division!

Our new home was to be in a tool tent. The supply corporal called Bolo (a name earned when he failed to qualify on the rifle range) brought out four cots, everyone with canvas splits. I was given a needle and thread to undertake the very difficult task of repairing a cot with canvas completely cut from one end to the other. After the job was finished, we went to evening chow where we ate standing up. Recently, I telephoned Rudy Thell, one of the four men from my unit that I had maintained contact with, and he said this was the lowest point in his Army life.

Going to bed, we discovered how cold it gets in the desert when the sun goes down. We came from comparative luxury with brand new facilities to the worst the army could offer—our drinking water came from lister bags (canvas bags with spigots).

We were not alone, as many soldiers encountered similar harsh conditions during the US Army's extraordinary efforts in creating fifty-plus new divisions to accommodate the war. In *Commander-in-Chief,* Eric Larabee describes the new Division process.

"General McNair invented the scheme for creating new divisions. Seventy-five days before the date of activation, he and General Marshall would appoint the Commanding General and two Brigadiers. These three (with advice from Marshall and McNair) would choose their principal subordinates.

"These officers would be sent to Command and General Staff school at Fort Leavenworth, Kansas for refresher courses. A "Parent" unit would be picked from existing divisions to provide a skeleton core. The 79th received a Cadre from the 4th Division. This Cadre could be as many as 185 officers and 1200 enlisted men for a division of 14,000. The remainder were filled with the product of basic training and the service schools. Some divisions were gutted several times, over the protest of their commanders, when their system got moving, it could product three or four new divisions a month.

"This training program also set up at the infantry school at Fort Benning, Georgia, taught thirty different courses to over 50,000 officers and 25,000 enlisted men. Courses in the different training schools covered motor vehicles, air invasion, radio repair, artillery mechanics, explosives, mines and booby traps. In addition to 63,000 officers candidates to 2nd Lt. The schools of the other combat arms: armored, antiaircraft, field and coastal artillery, cavalry, parachute and tank destroyer—a total of 138,000 officers, 136,000 officer candidates, and 295,000 enlisted men were graduated." [10]

BACKGROUND OF THE 79th INFANTRY DIVISION

In the autumn of 1918, American divisions overseas were requested to submit designs for a distinctive identifying insignia to be worn on the left shoulder. The 79th combat history until then had been quite brief, and confined to the Lorraine sector of the front in France. The blue and white "croix de Lorraine" was adopted as a symbol of triumph dating back to the 15th century and recognized the civilized world over. Thus, from the sector where it made military history by its assault and capture of Montfaucon during the Meuse-Argonne drive in the closing stages of World War I, the division derived both a patch and a new name.[11] This patch was well received as the symbol of France.

The 79th Infantry Division was reactivated on June 15th, 1942 at Camp Pickett, Virginia. On April 3rd, 1942, Major General Ira T. Wyche, Commanding General, accompanied by a staff of twenty-two officers from the Fourth Infantry Division reported to Fort Leavenworth, Kansas, for a month course of

---

[10] Larrabee 114, 119, 120
[11] Cross of Lorraine 7

training for "Officers of the New Divisions." One month later they proceeded to Camp Pickett, Virginia, where the new division was to be organized. Basic training at Camp Pickett, Virginia, and further training at Camp Blanding, Florida, was then followed by two months of maneuvers and other vigorous training in Tennessee. The division was then sent to Camp Laguna, Arizona, for three months of desert maneuvers. Camp Laguna had almost no facilities, as its sole purpose was to give the participating troops the most difficult kind of existence imaginable.

There were rows of tents stretching for miles in which the men slept and lived. Others housed kitchens, hospitals, and officers quarters. The only wooden buildings were for shower and wash rooms. [12]

We arrived at Camp Laguna when the days were warm and the nights were cold. Since the division had completed the desert maneuvers, there was little formal training going on. One day I had guard duty at the stockade, which consisted of chain link fence and tents in the middle. The Sergeant of the Guard warned me that these were dangerous men. When we got on the train to Camp Phillips, three of those dangerous men rode in the same car with me. I found them to be relatively good men who ran afoul of the system—Andrew Benson, a Swedish-Indian mixture; Dunham, a truck driver from New Jersey; and Clancy, a guardhouse lawyer from Chicago.

I was assigned to the 3rd Platoon, Company A. In a June 15, 2003 Washington Post article, Thomas Ricks wrote an interesting and very on-point article about men as they are assigned to their divisions:

——————————————
[12] History of the 313th 41

"Nor do they stop to talk—troops from another division might as well be from another world. In the military, your squad is your family, your platoon is your neighborhood and your company is your town. Beyond that, anyone else is pretty much a stranger." [13]

Ruby Thell and I were assigned KP duty on Thanksgiving Day. We had a good dinner of turkey and all the trimmings. I thought the pots and pans would never end. It was a new experience to wash them out in the open.

Each company trained a barber. Our barber was Jesus (Chico) Diaz, a Cuban kid. No matter what kind of haircut one requested, he gave everyone the same kind, one he called a "treem." In one of our last formations in the U.S., before shipping overseas, Lt. Warga asked Chico, "What do you think of the army?" To which Chico replied "The army is all right, it's the people that are in it..." (the actual words used are not fit to print!).

ON TO CAMP PHILLIPS

On December 8, 1943, we left Camp Laguna on a troop train headed for Camp Phillips, Kansas. The trip took four days through five western states—Arizona, New Mexico, Texas, Oklahoma, and Kansas. One of the two real characters in Company A was Bolo Cappella, a tool corporal and former employee of Barnum & Bailey Circus. He was a dice roller, and on the first night on the train he won $1,000 shooting craps. Three of us privates were shooting dice for pennies. He laughed at us and showed us the money he had won. He got back into the craps game but eventually lost it all. He then borrowed a dollar from someone and got into the penny ante game.

---

[13] Thomas E. Ricks. "On Patrol in Sweltering Baghdad a Platoon Turns up the Heat." Washington Post June 15, 2003

4

Camp Phillips, Kansas

After living in desert tents with none of the facilities that made army life bearable, everyone was glad to be back in civilization. Camp Phillips had modern services, clubs, post exchanges, churches and theaters. It was within fifteen miles of Salina, Kansas, a city of 25,000 people. The barracks were large one-story buildings, with oak floors and ample living space. The heating system consisted of three coal burning stoves situated at both ends and one in the center of the building. Near the stove it was too hot; I, fortunately, was about twenty-five feet from the stove.

The latrines and shower room were in a large building nearby. This meant cold runs to the latrine on the cold nights. The day room, supply room and company offices were in one large building. The kitchen and dining room were also in one building.

The company day room contained an old phonograph, several writing tables, and an old sofa or two. The record collection consisted of two records: *"No Letter Today"* and *"Born to Lose and Now I'm Losing You."* These two played over and over, so I can still sing the words today.

Upon our arrival, the division commanding general issued a statement that the fundamental purpose of our stay at Camp Phillips was to engage in an extensive period of winter training necessary to comply with "Preparation For Overseas Movement" requirements.

Winter training began almost immediately with forced marches where we jogged 500 paces then walked 500 paces. We covered five miles in sub-freezing weather at fifteen minutes per mile. The cold temperatures tightened our leg muscles and made them sore.

Several days were spent on the rifle range and the 1000-inch range on the thirty caliber heavy machine gun. I noticed a relaxed attitude with a lot of joking and carrying on. When I was in the pits, the men were told Lt. Warga was shooting. They marked his hits all over the target and then waived the flag (Maggie's Drawers) to indicate he missed the target. The men shot sharpshooter or expert when they got down to serious shooting, qualifying on the 1000-inch indoor range with heavy thirty caliber machine guns. After much practice, I was determined to hit all of the moving targets. I was the second-best-shooting sharpshooter.

As part of the aircraft identification program, we spent several days studying German and American airplanes. One night, we took a visual test. Planes were shown on a screen for a long moment and then we would identify the planes by name on paper. The room was hot and the pace was slow, so I put my head down for just a minute or two. The next thing I knew, the Captain said, "Wake that man and make him stand up." I got up with much laughter. The test continued and when the scores were posted, I was the only man that got every answer right. My experiences at Camp Phillips were as varied as the men I encountered. I first met Private Clancy when I guarded him in the stockade in Camp Laguna, AZ, and I got to know him well in Camp Phillips. He was chronically AWOL and refused to soldier. During the Tennessee Maneuvers, he dropped a bar of ivory soap in a stream. As it floated away, he followed it, later telling the military court that the next thing he knew, he was in Chicago. He was assigned permanent KP, working only at mealtime. In March 1944, a new regulation passed concerning dishonorable discharges that stated any soldier with a minimum number of days of good time could receive a general discharge instead of a dishonorable discharge. Since Private Clancy had served ninety days of good time at Camp Phillips and elsewhere, he was the first man to be discharged under the new regulation. His name and picture were in the newspapers—a guardhouse lawyer and a complete goof-off, honored by the army. I never saw a happier man or a bigger smile than I did the day he left camp, a day or two before we shipped out for overseas.

Each night, two men were selected to guard a Bailey bridge equipment location near Camp Phillips. One night, a West Virginia hillbilly named Buck and I were given the duty to watch the equipment in a guard shack with a leaky roof. We had just gone to bed when a downpour came. The roof leaked a regular torrent. Buck scouted round and found a horse barn nearby. We gathered our blankets and ran for it. I got under the blanket, wet clothes and all. By morning my clothes were dry. Buck, on the other hand, took off his clothing before getting under the blankets. In the morning his clothing was still wet and almost frozen. He started a fire, but he was still wet and shivering when our relief came. The moral of the story: If you get wet in cold weather and you can't dry your clothing, get in bed and your body heat will do the job.

One day, we ate lunch in a rocky wooded area near a large concrete pillbox site to be constructed in a former cow pasture. Someone noticed a rabbit, and one of the men ran it down. We then discovered an entire family of rabbits living under some large rocks. They were running in all directions, but when it was over we had ten or more rabbits to skin and cook for dinner.

Christmas Eve was spent in the Protestant chapel and was a melancholy evening. This was my first Christmas away from home, but for everyone else it was the second Christmas away from home. The Christmas Day menu included soup, roast turkey, gravy, mashed potatoes, candied sweet potatoes, peas, olives, mincemeat and cherry pies, nuts, ice cream, and coffee. The somber conversation reflected the mens' time away from home, now over two years.

As part of the Christmas celebration, a dinner dance was held on Saturday evening. Local girls were bused in from Salina for the occasion. Most of the men started to party early, so that by the time dinner was over, fights broke out. As a result of the fighting, the girls from Salina went home early. I talked to some of the girls and apologized for the bad behavior of the men.

A favorite barracks game consisted of throwing a bayonet at the selected soldier's feet. The winner was the soldier that permitted the bayonet to stick in the floor closest to his feet without flinching.

Five or six of the older NCOs had their wives staying in Salina. They would spend nights and weekends with their wives in town. One Saturday, we had a formal review with the officer's wives in attendance. The first sergeant, a tall lean man from Mississippi, yelled at a private late in joining the formation, "You're running like a jug of piss." He then turned around to report the company assembled only to discover the officers' wives standing there with red faces.

Furloughs began on December 1943, and after several false starts, I received a seven-day leave in early March. My brother Milf was on leave also so we had a good time together. The remaining days were filled with rifle drills and exercises. New duffel bags and other equipment were issued to prepare us for the overseas assignment.

Finally the day came for us to be shipped out by Pullman on March 30, 1944. We were headed for places unknown. The train was routed to Kansas City, Joliet, and Chicago, Illinois, Gary, Indiana, Toledo, Ohio, following the shoreline to Lake Erie in Cleveland, Ohio and then on to Buffalo and Binghamton, New York, then into Massachusetts to Camp Miles Standish.

CAMP MILES STANDISH

The train pulled into the new camp at 1:00 a.m. Troop trains side-tracked to freight trains and passenger trains. We received coffee and doughnuts. Camp Miles Standish was located near Taunton MA, on sandy soil with an abundance of scrub pine. The barracks were typical government issue. We spent some some in training, but mostly waited for the day we loaded onto the boat. If the men were apprehensive or fearful about going overseas to combat, it did not show. But had they voiced their real feelings they would have been diminished in the eyes of one another. [14]

The day before we embarked, one private caught "gangplank fever" and deserted. He said he was not going overseas, and he didn't. The day came to leave with an early wakeup. We put our belongings into new duffel bags and loaded them onto trucks. The ride to the railroad station was not long. We detrucked and caught a streamliner of the New Haven line. After a half-hour ride, we pulled into Boston and ended up on the docks. Red Cross ladies met us with coffee and doughnuts. When we got our first look at the *Explorer*, most of us looked forward to this great adventure. Laughing and joking, we struggled with our duffel bags, rifles, and belongings.

───────────────

[14] Kindsvatter 68

UNITED STATES SHIP

U.S.A.T.
EXPLORER

Length, overall: 4731"	Gross tons: 6,736	Propulsion: Turbine
Beam: 660"	Speed (knots): 16 1/2	Passengers: 2,129
Draft: 27'1"	Radius (miles): 20,000	Cargo: (cu. ft.) 127,340

Built in 1939 by Bethlehem Steel Company,
Quincy, Massachusetts

Operated during World War II by
American Export Lines. Inc.

The *EXPLORER* operated as a C3 type cargo vessel for nearly four Years before becoming a troopship. As a freighter, she made many voyages to various areas in the war effort, two of the longest being: (1) from Baltimore in December 1942, through the Panama Canal, to Fremantle (Australia), Shatt-al-Arab (Iraq), Bombay (India), Colombo (Ceylon), Calcutta and Vizagapatam (India), and return via Fremantle and the Canal Zone to New York in late May 1943: (2) From New York in early June to Oran, Gibraltar, and Casablanca, back to New York between early August and early November, 1943.

Leaving Boston on 6 November, the ship made five voyages to the Clyde before May 1944, returning in each case to either Boston or New York. On 13 May, she departed from Boston to the Mersey, Liverpool, Cardiff (Wales) and Belfast (Ireland).

Returning to Boston in late July, the vessel made another voyage to the Clyde, followed by one to Cherbourg and the United Kingdom, one from New York to Bristol and Avonmouth, and one from New York to the Mersey, Liverpool, and Belfast.

From the latter port, *Explorer* returned to New York in January 1945. Ten days later, she proceeded to Europe for five months shuttle service between Le Havre and Southampton. On 6 June 1945, *Explorer* left Le Havre for her trip back to the United States. She blew two boilers on the way and didn't arrive in Hampton Roads (Norfolk) until 16 June.

Explorer made a voyage from Norfolk to Le Havre in July and one from Boston to Le Havre in August. V.J. Day having occurred, the Explorer was dispatched to the Pacific, via the Panama Canal, and proceeded directly to Manila, from where she returned to Seattle in October. Touching at San Francisco for repairs, the vessel went to Nagova, Japan, and from there sailed for the Canal Zone and New York, where she arrived 3 January 1946 and was released from troopship service and returned to commercial service, to the Export Lines, on 15 October 1962.

She was placed on reserve on the James River and sold to the Boston Metals Company for scrap on 9 April 1969. She was removed on 28 April 1969 and towed to Baltimore, Maryland when she was cut up for scrap.

5

The Explorer

The American wartime shipbuilding program started in 1938[15] with the goal of building 50 ships per year. The U.S. Maritime commission, headed by Adm. Emory S. Land, was responsible for building the ships. By 1945, the shipbuilding program had produced 5,800 vessels, mostly large cargo carriers and tankers with 56 million tons capacity in order to carry 65 million tons of oil and gasoline around the world. We built more than 600 new tankers. This new shipbuilding was accomplished by increasing the number of shipyards to 70 and by shortening the number of days to build a standard merchantman (10,000 tons, The Liberty or Victory ships) from

---

[15] The 1938 Supplemental also covered battleships and carriers for the Navy, new divisions for the Army and B-17s and P-38s for the Army Air Corps.
[16] Murray & Millett 536

105 to 56 days.[16]

David Kennedy described the process as "The many men and a handful of women who made the Patrick Henry toiled for 355 days. Just six months later in mid 1942, shipyard gangs could make a liberty ship from keel-lying to launch in less than a third of the time, 105 days by 1943. Construction crews were splashing liberty ships from scratch in forty-one days. Later on they would make one in just seventeen days"[17]

After walking up the gangplank, we noticed the guns and the deck area. The next step was down the ladder into the hold. Bunks were stacked five high. I picked the bottom bunk and proceeded to dump my duffel bag and rifle on it. We had to find room to sleep amidst this mess.

After putting the bunk in order, we visited the latrine, or head, in navy talk. The toilets had no seats, which made for some cold sitting. Next we went into the mess hall of tables. We stood for meals; continuous serving was necessary to feed the men two meals per day. If memory serves me right, we were served at 9:35 a.m. and 5:30 p.m.

We then ventured out on the deck to look around the Boston harbor. The ship pulled anchor about 3:00 p.m. and sailed out of the harbor. I considered this the first day of the grand adventure for this small town boy from Minnesota. There were many ships in the harbor and we enjoyed the view of the Boston skyline.

After an hour or so, we cleared the harbor and sailed into the Atlantic Ocean. We later discovered there were fifty ships

[17] Kennedy 660

in the Boston convoy (a full half of the invasion convoy). The next day we joined the fifty ships of the New York convoy.

The battleship Texas was with us, as well as troop ships, freighters and tankers. The tankers and freighters traveled on the inside and the troop transports on the outside. The US would rather lose a troopship than a tanker or freighter, since petroleum, munitions, and supplies were more valuable than the lives of the men. Our ship was the last vessel on the left side of the convoy, commonly referred to as "The Coffin Corner."

A ring of destroyers and sub chasers surrounded the convoy. I learned that the N.Y. convoy sunk a sub near the N.Y. harbor. We could feel the blast when depth charges exploded. The charge almost threw you out of your bunk. The ship nearest ours on the inside carried a load of WACs. We would wave at them when they were on the deck.

The first night—Holy Thursday—a Protestant service was held in the mess hall on board ship. I met the chaplain; a young man named Rasmussen, from a town twenty-five miles from my hometown of Lyle, Minnesota. I discovered that I knew his parents and younger sister. (Note: I later met him at a service in a Lutheran church in Alsace. The Lutheran Magazine reported his death at age ninety-four.)

The seas were never so rough as to cause seasickness, but I wasn't comfortable below deck in the stuffy troop compartment. I was offered a job working in the navy mess, but turned it down because I wanted to spend fifteen hours a day topside. After breakfast, I would take my position sitting on a post used to tie the boat up to dock and remained there until 10 p.m. or so. It was warm and relatively calm for the first three days, which made for pleasant outside sitting. A steady stream of men, twenty or more, came just to talk. These sessions gave me a chance for some informal counseling on the problems and challenges that lay ahead. A number of the men faced the coming combat with apprehension as to their survival. Most thought casualties were something that happened to others, and they would not be harmed.

I never tired of watching the ocean and the feeling that the waves had been rolling for ages. I wondered whether these same waves broke against the Pilgrim ships 400 years ago. One day I would sit on the east side facing the 100 ships in the convoy, and the next day on the west side watching the ocean and destroyers and sub chasers bobbing up and down in the waves.

On the fifth or sixth day out, an infamous North Atlantic storm hit us. The convoy increased the distance between ships and reduced the speed from 14 knots to around 10 knots. Fifty-foot high waves would lift the ship and then drop it so you could hear the propeller straining to climb the next wave. If one were unfortunate enough to come on deck when the ship dropped, one would go careening down—only to be stopped by the guardrail.

Most men got seasick and were green in their misery, spending most days below deck. One evening the meal, consisting of corned beef hash and poached eggs, made someone sick before I arrived. I managed to eat about half of the meal before I had to go above deck for fresh air. I was the only man in the company who showed up for every meal. After three days, the storm subsided and the convoy resumed its speed of 14 knots. Every now and then, sub chasers would drop depth charges that almost knocked you out of bed.

The next eight days flew by as most men became accustomed to the roll of the ocean. The number dropping by to visit me increased steadily. The cold wind was transformed into a spring-like wind. It was a very pleasant experience to sit by the hour and watch the sky and the waves.

EUROPEAN ARRIVAL

Eventually, Northern Ireland came into view and then the ship entered the Firth of Clyde into the River Clyde in Grenoch, the Port of Glasgow. We anchored in the harbor in the morning to witness a rustic scene. The City of Grenoch is located between low mountains. Sea gulls were in abundance, and children and a few old codgers waved to us. I couldn't help thinking of the thousands of immigrants that had sailed from this port to new lands. Now thousands of GIs were embarking to help in the war effort.*

We watched large troop ships come by. We saw the West Point, painted in camouflage colors of tan and grey. In the middle of the afternoon, small passenger boats came to take us to shore. Each boat carried roughly twenty-five soldiers with duffel bags. On the boat I was on, a man offered cigarettes to the man next to him. That pack was passed around the boat and when it was returned to the owner, it was empty. We unloaded from the boat and boarded a train on a siding to take us to Leek in Staffordshire County.

*Note: Pastor Campbell McKinnon and his wife were from Grenoch. He was an Assistant Pastor at Luther Place Memorial Church in Washington, DC in the early 1960s.

6

England

The train, with its shrill whistle and small engine by American standards, was otherwise very good. I especially enjoyed the low mountains and colorful heather in the sunlight of a perfect April day. As the train went through a tunnel, what did we see but a couple having sex less than fifty feet from the train track. The men in the train cheered and hooted to encourage the man to dig deeper. The poor man pulled his partner's dress over him and tried to hide by digging into the ground.

I enjoyed the green surroundings of the towns and cities passing by. Eventually, the train pulled into Leek, a town in Staffordshire in the midlands.

Our barracks, formerly used by the British army, had bunk beds and modern toilet facilities. A large rifle rack containing eighty or more rifles stood in the middle of the barracks. Night after night the pubs of Leek were filled with US troops, drinking freely of English beer and ale, singing English and American songs, and mingling with Tommies and civilians. After the day's work was done, the men made every night into a holiday.

English girls frequented the pubs and dancehalls and provided good company to men who were looking for female companionship. Many meetings turned into sexual relationships, and the soldiers often carried pictures of British girls in their wallets. In fact, during combat, when a GI was killed, all pictures were removed so that pictures of an English girl would not be sent home. For many of the men, sex was the object in dating English girls. The girls told the GI's if they had sex lying down, they would be considered whores, while sex standing up was okay and seldom resulted in pregnancy. Often walking along a dark street, we encountered two forms in a doorway with the man pumping away.

The severe food shortage in England was strongly impressed upon the troops. We were warned not to buy food or meals in town, nor to accept hospitality of civilians who offered food.

What helped most in relieving the food shortage, however, was the arrival of the American invasion forces. GI's brought food and charity in abundance, sharing their food with many women and children. The Army was confident that it could provide the soldiers with food in abundance by calculating the toilet tissue allowance per soldier stationed in England at 22.5 sheets per day. The British soldier's ration was three sheets per day.[18]

As mentioned above, many men spent time in the pubs. They drank ale and stout unaware that the alcohol content was 10% to 15%, a lot higher than the 3.2% alcohol content found in American beer. One man bragged that he was going to get drunk on a Saturday night and come home and piss on the rifles in the rifle rack. One Saturday night he did just that after filling up on beer and ale. He spent Sunday cleaning some fifty or more rifles, which was a smelly job.

Our training was aimed to further physical training—we endured five-, ten- and fifteen-mile marches. On one forced march, we were required to wear raincoats, resulting in wet, perspired clothing.

---

[18] Murray & Millett 530

Army standards mandated that a single Bailey bridge was to be no longer than 170 feet. The River Dee was 185 feet wide. We assembled the bridge piece by piece and pushed it across. Sure enough, the bridge collapsed into the river. The trick was to decouple the bridge without hurting anyone. One large former coal miner poked the bolt out with a sledgehammer and the bridge dropped into the river, hitting him with a glancing blow. I don't remember how we pulled the bridge out of the river, but I do remember that it was a backbreaking job.

The evening before building the bridge, a large procession from a local Church of England appeared on the riverbank. They were celebrating Whitsuntide (Pentacost) with banners and chanting hymns. I was very impressed with the pageantry in the park-like setting near the River Dee.

We found the British people to be very friendly. The kids chased us asking for gum, chum and other candies. I went to church every Sunday at various churches. Once I went with a friend, the company clerk and fellow preacher's son, who had befriended a family who owned a dairy. We were invited out to Sunday dinner and accepted reluctantly because we had been instructed not to eat out while in England. That family used a week or more of rationing coupons to give us a nice meal that included homemade ice cream—the first ice cream they had made since 1940.

The days went by faster than I realized. We were expecting a call to mobilize for the invasion at any day. As a climax for the events of May, Lt. General George S. Patton addressed the officers and sergeants in the division. The NCOs reported back to the troops the essentials of his fiery, profanity-laced speech. Patton told them they would be called to lead men against a determined and vicious enemy. He ended his remarks by praising the division, whom he predicted would give a good account of themselves in the combat ahead.[19]

Note: This speech, reported in the British Press, was part of a misinformation plan to mislead the Germans to believe that Patton would lead the U.S. Third Army invasion near Pas-de-Calais. Operation Fortitude intentionally misled the Germans into believing that the main invasion would be led by General Patton. The German General Staff fell for the hoax and expected the invasion in the Pas-de-Calais area and not Normandy, which might have made the difference in the first days after the invasion.[20]

New equipment was issued: trucks jeeps, bulldozers, etc. We were also issued machine guns, bazookas, and all the equipment assigned to a company of combat engineers. The men of Company A had been awaiting this big moment for so long that they were almost eager for the time to come. On May 30, the order came. Everything was readied for a long convoy to an unknown destination.

WRONG GLASSES

Just before we left for the encampment overlooking the Bristol Channel, the doctors checked my eyes and issued new glasses.

When I put them on, I couldn't see as well as with my existing glasses and immediately realized that they were the wrong prescription. When I complained to the doctor, he dismissed my concern and replied that the prescription was correct and I would just have to get used to them.

---

[19] History of 313th Infantry 66
[20] Weigley 73, 74

After two days trial, I threw them away and spent the year in combat without glasses. While I need glasses for reading and to prevent eyestrain, my overall vision did not require glasses.

When the war ended in May 1945 and doctors checked us out, a doctor reminded me that I needed to wear glasses and proceeded to bawl me out for not wearing them. I replied that I was not going to wear glasses that didn't fit. New glasses issued were the correct prescription, so I wore glasses again.

CAMPING OVER THE BRISTOL CHANNEL

On June 1, 1944, A Company, 304th Combat Engineers Battalion left Leek, England for a camp overlooking the Bristol Channel, in one long convoy. The captain's command car was followed by a Mack truck carrying the D-6 dozer, an air-compressor truck, a kitchen truck, and platoon vehicles such as jeeps and trucks. The convoy speed was set by the slowest vehicle. It was quite a sight to see twelve 2½-ton trucks, each filled with thirteen GIs. We roared through villages large and small while crowds lined the streets, waving and wishing us luck. The children called out for gum and candy. The English people were amazed by the vast number of vehicles of every kind that traveled in mile after mile of convoys.

John Keegan's *"Six Armies in Normandy"* described the scene.

"More striking were the number, size, and elegance of the vehicles in which they paraded about the country in stately convoys—The Americans traveled in magnificent, gleaming, olive green, pressed steel, four wheel drive, juggernauts decked out—with winches, towing cable and fire extinguishers."[21]

Late in the day, we arrived at our campsite overlooking the Bristol Channel and immediately proceeded to set up camp—pitching our pup tents and digging latrines. The army provided the food (hiring and training 4,500 new army cooks) and services for the marshaling area, which required 54,000 men. We were sealed off from the outside world.

England outdid herself in the clear, cool days and nights. Eighth Air Force planes came over every night. We counted the planes by the green lights on each plane. We had our 30-caliber heavy machine guns set up. The guns had been issued to us in Leek but had not been test-fired yet.

One night, for no apparent reason, Haradan got out of bed and started to fire at the B-17's overhead. The captain came running in his underwear shorts, and stopped the firing—yelling at Haradan. Then the captain reduced Haradan from the rank of T/5 to Private.

The night of June 5, 1944 at about 11:00 p.m., we saw planes flying overhead—a line of C-47's about thirty-five miles wide and 350 miles long. We could see the red and green lights of 822 C-47's dropping 13,000 paratroopers.[22]

As John Keegan describes the experience, "The sight was "extraordinary," "breathtaking" and "majestic"...as Ridgeway

---

[21] Keegan 11 – 12
[22] Larrabee 45

recalled, with the V of V's only 150 feet from wing tip to wing tip and no lights to guide them except little lavender lights you could hardly see, only a thousand feet from one flight of nine aircraft to the next and with as many as five hundred aircraft on the same track, it was extremely easy to overrun the plane ahead."[23]

We awoke early on June 6th and listened to the radio for news of the invasion. We spent the morning huddled around the radio listening to the BBC. Many of the men were deep in thought—apprehension combined with a hope that someone else will die and not them.

I don't remember how we spent the days until June 13th when we left for the Port of Falmouth. Live ammunition, gas masks, and fatigues were issued. The fatigues were specially treated with a chemical that would protect us from a gas attack. American money was changed into French invasion currency.

The 304th Combat Engineers-Battalion pulled out of camp on the morning of June 13th, 1944 in one long convoy headed for the Port of Falmouth. We arrived early in the morning to join one of fifty lines of vehicles. Each line consisted of vehicles of every kind—jeeps, trucks, tanks, artillery guns, ambulances, etc. The line moved slowly and finally we reached the place where the LST (landing ship tank) was docked. We rode up the ramp and parked on the deck. There were about 600 men and fifty vehicles on the LST 410. The LST 410 was a British ship, so no pictures of it are available.

---

[23] Keegan 11-12

LST Ship

Departure was in early afternoon. Clearing the port, we saw 400-500 vessels of every kind steaming for Normandy. Strangely, the English Channel was smooth as glass. Every other time I crossed the Channel, the voyage was rough with choppy waters. I enjoyed watching the ships filling the channel as far as the eye could see. Most of the men kept their thoughts to themselves. We arrived off the Normandy coast by sunset. The sky was red and the water was tinted pink. In the early evening, we anchored off Utah Beach. Since Normandy observed double daylight time, sunset that day in June was 11:00 p.m.

The battleship Texas was anchored within a mile of us. When she fired her 14" guns, the blast lifted the blankets off of us as we slept under our truck on deck. A German plane flew up the beach, strafing and dropping one bomb. While we were sleeping, it started to rain and since my blanket was over a seam in the deck where water ran down, it became totally soaked. Allied commanders had 15,766 aircraft of all kinds available to support the D-Day operation. Each airplane was painted with the black and white stripes to identify the planes in an obvious manner. These stripes made identification easy, so as to avoid planes being shot down by accident.

UNITED STATES SHIP

LST

The History of an LST

The preliminary plans initially called for an LST 280 feet in length; but in January 1942, the Bureau of Ships discarded these drawings in favor of specifications for a ship 290 feet long. Within a month, final working plans were developed which further stretched the overall length to 328 feet and called for a 50-foot beam and minimum draft to 3 feet 9½ inches.

The LST could carry a 2,100-ton load of tanks and vehicles. The larger dimensions also permitted the designers to increase the width of the bow door opening and ramp from 12-14 feet and thus accommodate most Allied vehicles. The keel of the first LST was laid down on 10 June 1942 at Newport News, Virginia. The need for LSTs was urgent and the program enjoyed a high priority throughout the war. In some instances, heavy industry plants such as steel fabrication yards were converted for LST construction. This posed the problem, of getting the completed ships from the inland building yards to deep water. The chief obstacles were bridges.

The Navy successfully undertook the modification of bridges and, through a "Terry Command" of Navy crews, transported the newly constructed ships to coastal ports for fitting out. Of the 1,051 LSTs built during World War II,

670 were constructed by five major inland builders. By 1943 the construction time for an LST had been reduced to four months.

From their combat debut in the Solomon Islands in June 1943 until the end of hostilities in August 1945, the LST performed a vital service in World War II. Throughout the war, LSTs demonstrated a remarkable capacity to absorb punishment and survive. The LSTs suffered few losses in proportion to their number and the scope of their operations. Although the LST was considered a valuable target by the enemy, only 26 were lost due to enemy action.

In 1944 Winston Churchill said "What is this ship called, that is holding the invasion of Europe up," and Ike said. "It's an LST." The LST was the ship that brought World War II to a close, no other ship could put men, equipment and supplies ashore like an LST.

Following World War II most of the LSTs were either sold for commercial use or sold for scrap. Several were placed in the reserve fleet, only a few remained in active service. In 1950 the Korean War came along. The United States recalled several back to service. LSTs took names of counties on 1 July 1950. They remained in service and were used in the Vietnam War, transporting troops and cargo. Several were used as a mother ship for the Riverean Force in the Delta. The last of the World War II, LSTs left the service in the late 1970s. Most were either sold or given to governments around the world and are still in use today.

The Newport class came and went. The last one was placed out of service in 2003. There are no active LSTs in the United States Navy now and none on the drawing board. Air-Cruiser vehicles and Hellos put men ashore in today's military.

SUPREME HEADQUARTERS
ALLIED EXPEDITIONARY FORCE

Soldiers, Sailors and Airmen of the Allied Expeditionary Force!

You are about to embark upon the Great Crusade, toward which we have striven these many months. The eyes of the world are upon you. The hopes and prayers of liberty loving people everywhere march with you. In company with our brave Allies and brothers-in-arms on other Fronts, you will bring about the destruction of the German war machine, the elimination of Nazi tyranny over the oppressed peoples of Europe, and security for ourselves in a free world.

Your task will not be an easy one. Your enemy is well trained, well equipped and battle-hardened. He will fight savagely.

But this is the year 1944! Much has happened since the Nazi triumphs of 1940-41. The United Nations have inflicted upon the Germans great defeats, in open battle, man-to-man. Our air offensive has seriously reduced their strength in the air and their capacity to wage war on the ground. Our Home Fronts have given us an overwhelming superiority in weapons and munitions of war, and placed at our disposal great reserves of trained fighting men. The tide has turned! The free men of the world are marching together to Victory!

I have full confidence in your courage, devotion to duty and skill in battle. We will accept nothing less than full Victory!

Good Luck! And let us all beseech the blessing of Almighty God upon this great and noble undertaking.

Dwight Eisenhower

Army Battle Organization

First Army   Lt. General Omar Bradley
VII Corps   Major General J. Lawton Collins
Composed of 4th, 9th, 79th and 90th Division

THE 79th INFANTRY DIVISION TABLE OF ORGANIZATION

Headquarters and Headquarters Company

79th Reconnaissance Troops
313th Infantry Regiment
314th Infantry Regiment
315th Infantry Regiment
304th Engineer Combat Battalion
304th Medical Battalion

79th Division Artillery – HQ and HQ Battery

310th Field Artillery Battalion
311th Field Artillery Battalion
312th Field Artillery Battalion
904th Field Artillery Battalion
79th Infantry Division Special Troops
779th Ordnance LM Co.
79th Signal Company
79th Division Platoon
79th Division Band

Each Division had units assigned:

The 463rd AAA Automatic Weapons Battalion
The 749th Tank Battalion
The 813th Tank Destroyer Battalion
Corps Artillery, such as long TOMS (155M Cannons),
    8" Howitzers, etc. were also assigned depending
    on need for additional artillery

7

Normandy Landing

The 463rd AAA Automatic Weapons Battalion; the 749th Tank Battalion; the 813th Tank Destroyer Battalion corps artillery, such as long TOMS (155M Cannons); 8" Howitzers, etc. were also assigned depending on need for additional artillery

As we off-loaded from the LST, we saw several hundred wounded men waiting for the trip back to England.

Steve Vogel's History of LST 325 writes:

"During return runs to England from Normandy, LST 325 was loaded with wounded U.S. soldiers, and the wardroom was turned into an operating room as Navy Corpsmen struggled to save lives. Many of the wounded died aboard ship, a memory that chokes up Kurz (an officer from 1943 to 1945) to the day. You wanted to get them back, but you couldn't, he said, on a sea that is rough, it was like a floating bed pan."

I had put this entirely out of my mind, until fifty years later when I looked out to the sea from Utah Beach during this flashback. It was so real that I was transported back fifty years for a moment or two.

Our trucks came off the LST in succession and moved across a gentle climb to the edge of the beach. Almost immediately, we came to an area that was flooded with water. I understood why the airborne division wanted to take the land beyond, so our infantrymen would not have to take the flooded areas. We noticed several collapsed parachutes in the water.

After the flooded area, we passed through a fairly large field enclosed by the hedgerows—row upon row of dirt and trees. Hedgerows presented a unique challenge for the army and those will be discussed in detail later in this chapter. We immediately noticed several downed gliders. Upon further investigation, we discovered that each glider had bullet holes and bloody bandages in them.

The first order of business was to dig slit trenches to sleep in and dig latrines. Rations were issued consisting of three vitamin and mineral enriched D bars per day. Cigarettes, candy and gum were issued later. Canteens were filled from five-gallon cans. The water was treated with chlorine since our systems were not used to local minerals and other impurities. Even so, most of us got loose bowels.

The double daylight time in western Europe meant darkness came at 11:00 p.m. The normal routine was to dig in if we were in a new area. We couldn't go to sleep until 12 a.m. and we all rotated serving two hours of guard duty. This system gave us five hours of sleep.

Whenever we moved from one site to another, I was constantly amazed that each unit was given a designated space to set up—even in the middle of the night. This must have taken a lot of planning to assign units as small as platoons.

The 79th Infantry Division went into combat almost two years to the day from its activation on June 15th, 1942. Two years later the division was trained to a high degree of combat efficiency. Raw recruits now were expert in infantry, artillery, engineers, etc. into a finely tuned infantry division.

Amos Wilder found two related reasons why esprit was a valuable motivator.

"First, soldiers who were proud of their outfit fought not only for their comrades and their self-respect but also because they had a standard of fighting excellence to uphold. Second, the soldier drew a significant measure of self-esteem in return. He belonged to a crack outfit, thus by association he too was an accomplished fighter." [24]

The men of the 79th Division were proud that their division was one of the best attack divisions in France. They were especially proud of the Cross of Lorraine patch. In fact, the 79th was the only division that served in all the armies in Europe (the 1st, 3rd, 7th, and 9th).

The men of the 304th Combat Engineers Battalion thought they were an elite combat engineers group. They prided themselves in a job well done in anything they undertook to do.

NORMANDY—CHERBOURG

In 1994 during a trip through the Normandy beaches to commemorate the 50th anniversary, I realized that the invasion area was a large area about sixty miles north to south. As soldiers during the war, we traveled from one place to another without realizing the size of the total area.

Hedgerows, or Bocage, were the main challenge. One cannot understand the Battle in Normandy without understanding the challenges of the hedgerows or Bocage.

---

[24] Wilder 145

Russell F. Weigley in Eisenhower's Lieutenants describes the Bocage.

"The Bocage is a hilly region extending south almost as far as the base of the Brittany Peninsula. In the Bocage, the hedgerows are ubiquitous. They have evolved over centuries, first planted by the Norman farmers as boundary markers, then retained out of custom, to protect field and flocks from the cold winds off the ocean and the Channel, and as a source of firewood. Their earthen parapets are from a meter to four meters high, on the average somewhat over a meter, and from about a third of a meter to more than a meter in thickness. Growing out of the walls are hedges of hawthorn, brambles, vines, and trees from a meter to five meters high, also adding an additional meter or so to the thickness. The hedgerows divide the whole Bocage into innumerable enclosures, some larger than a football field but most much smaller. Each hedgerow provided the Germans with a natural earthwork, the bushes on top offering a wealth of concealment for small arms and machine gun positions. Apart from the few main roads, passage among the hedgerows was a wagon trail, in effect sunken lanes, often overarched by the hedges and thus transformed into a labyrinth of covered ways, to conceal the defender and befuddle the attacker. Each hedgerow bounded field of the Bocage would tend to become a separate battleground, subject to conquest only by slow advances with rifles and grenades by infantrymen hugging the walls, with tank support useful but the overall situation a nightmare for mechanized forces, a dream for a defending army with the limited mobility of Germans' ordinary infantry and garrison divisions."[25]

---

[25] Weigley 51-52

The Germans formed garrison divisions for defending the fortifications off the beach. These divisions were not equipped for general infantry duties as they consisted of soldiers with limited mobility due to wounds and injuries.

Normandy was famous for its prize dairy herds. One distinctive memory was the sight of hundreds of dead Holstein cows with their legs in the air. Artillery and bombs killed 105,000 cows. The first use of the D-6 Bull Dozer was to dig large holes to bury the stinking cows.

Normandy is also famous for apple trees. During the war 300,000 apple trees were destroyed, thereby eliminating the region's cash crop. Company A stayed near St. Mere Eglise until the 15th of June when we moved to an area south of Valones to await a call to relieve the 90th Division for the drive toward Cherbourg.

A great Atlantic storm hit the beach on June 18th with driving rain and wind. It was nearly impossible to keep the water from coming through our two-man tents and into the foxholes even though we ditched around the tent. This storm not only halted unloading off the beach, it also destroyed the American Mulberry, a docking system made on sunken barges.[26] The Americans decided that the damage was irreparable, so we went back to the beaches for unloading supplies. By June 29th, a total of 7,000 tons of supplies had been unloaded at Utah Beach and 13,500 tons at Omaha Beach.

The call to our squad came during the afternoon of June 18th. When I heard the news, I found a private place and fell to my knees. I prayed for God to protect me and bring me through the battles unharmed. I added that if God would protect me, I

---

[26] Murray & Millett 425

would serve him for the rest of my life. My prayers were answered and I have tried to serve him faithfully ever since.

The Infantry jumped off at 5:00 a.m. on a rainy June 19th, 1944. The 313th Infantry, in division reserve, came through a lane near our area. The men appeared to be in a good mood, laughing and yelling. Each man, I am sure, thought he would be okay, that while others might be wounded or killed, he would not. I was reminded of a painting I have seen in the Smithsonian, of medieval knights going into battle with the sun shining and everyone looking forward to the coming victory. Each man carried a gas mask pouch. At the end of the first day, once the threat of gas attacks had been diminished, they were discarded, leaving thousands of masks littering the ground. We heard machine gun and rifle fire as well as artillery and mortar shells exploding. By that afternoon, ambulances and jeeps loaded with stretchers were passing us by.

DEALING WITH DEATH

On the day of June 19th, the 79th Division relieved the 90th Division and held the middle between the 4th and the 9th Division. The week before the June 19th invasion, the 90th Division retreated about a thousand yards. The first objective of 313th Regiment was to retake that thousand yards, which they did. The first squad of my platoon was given the job of picking up dead bodies. When we lifted the first body, his brains fell out all over my fatigues. Another body had his penis completely cut off by shrapnel. We picked up ten bodies or so, all of them blackened by the sun. We loaded them onto the truck and proceeded to the cemetery at Omaha Beach. We ate our lunch of K rations with dead bodies under our feet. The cemetery was a mass of dirt and mud, with open graves and bodies lying around. I had completely forgotten this incident until fifty years later, as I stood overlooking that awe-inspiring site. A flashback brought me back to the burial details fifty years earlier.

One Tuesday in August of 2003, while eating lunch at the senior center, I found myself back at the cemetery near Omaha Beach. This was the sixth flashback, which means this grim scene still haunts my memory bank to this day.

The peaceful feeling found visiting the cemetery today conceals the stark reality of those burials sixty years ago. Violent death was everywhere. It seemed that the dead soldiers' blood was crying from the ground as the blood of Abel's had cried out thousands of years earlier. Freshly dug graves filled the field. Soldiers worked to remove dog tags, billfolds, and personal items from the corpses and place them into body bags where they were dumped into holes. Nowhere did I see any chaplains or any religious ceremonies being performed. I later learned that the cemetery was dedicated before it opened.

While serving in a Chicago church, my father, a Lutheran pastor, was asked to conduct a funeral service for a Polish Catholic neighbor who had committed suicide. The Catholic Church refused to conduct the service, and when they asked my father, they asked him not to mention the suicide. My father replied that he preaches to the living, not the dead. Military chaplains worked in a similar fashion, serving the living at aide stations or with troops in the field. Therefore, there is no need for chaplains at the burial site.

Checking for mines was a common duty during this period. On June 20th, the first squad was detailed to check for mines along a main road with a lot of vehicle traffic. One man with the detector covered half the road and shoulders to the hedgerows; while another man probed with a bayonet whenever the detector picked up metal. A French farmer appeared with a bottle of cognac and two bottles of wine. He told us he buried them in 1940, and that he wanted to give them to the first Americans he saw. That wine was the best ever and the cognac was aged to perfection. As we passed the bottles around, mine detection became more of a fun game so we finally returned to our camping area because I couldn't find two sober men to man the detectors.

Normandy was famous for hard cider and calvados (distilled cider similar to white lightning or tequila). Each farm complex of buildings had barrels of cider. Soldiers often filled their canteens with hard cider, and afterwards they often left the corks off allowing the cider run out. Cider gave soldiers diarrhea and calvados produced stupor in the men.

Each 2½-ton truck had a radio that we used to listen to the Foreign Service of the BBC. News was given at dictation speed and one soldier in each unit was responsible for copying the news and sharing it with others. Berlin Sally made nightly appearances on air. One day she welcomed the 79th Division and claimed they would be destroyed. The next day she played American music of the big bands. We also listened to the French Resistance, mostly in code.

"Bedcheck Charlie" was the name of a German airplane that flew over our front line each evening at dusk. The American lines were easy to see due to the metal cans lying around that reflected light. One or two German guns would fire all night to keep American soldiers awake. American counter battery would answer. We would count the seconds from seeing the flash at firing until the artillery hit in American lines. Figuring that sound travels 1,090 feet per second, we could determine how far away the German artillery was.

On June 19th, 1944, the VII Corps was under the leadership of General Lawton Collins (Lightning Joe), who had combat experience in Guadalcanal. The battle situation involved the

79th Division replacing the 90th Division into the line with the 4th Division on the right, the 79th Division in the middle, and the 9th Division on the left. All positioned to attack northward toward Cherbourg by the morning of June 19th.

By Russell Weigley's account, General Eddy's 9th had little problem, the 79th had a more difficult time, but this organized reserve division, commanded from May 1942 to date by Major General Ira T. Wyche of the West Point Class of 1911, was not only luckier than the 90th in quality of its opposition, but also from the start well brought up. The worst problem facing the VII Corps was the bad weather![27]

Good progress was made and the infantry unit achieved their objectives. The battalions of the 313th Infantry ran out of ammunition by the afternoon, due to shooting rifles and mortars into the corners of each hedgerow. The next objective was the high ground south of Cherbourg. The main attack started along the Valoones-Cherbourg Highway where advancing troops ran into a blown bridge. The third platoon was called to build a temporary bridge by cutting down trees with a large two-man chain saw, placing them across the stream, and topping it off with a layer of gravel. The goal of the combat engineers is to build just enough to get the infantry across. We did not worry that the stream would eventually wash out the temporary bridge.

Late that afternoon, the 1st Battalion ran out of ammunition and re-supply vehicles could not get across the double track railroad. Again, combat engineers were called in to blow the track up to let vehicles through. The noise of Sherman tanks traveling a sunken lane not fifty feet from where we slept in our foxholes filled the night of the 21st. The clanking sound

---

[27] Weigley 102

was so loud and prolonged that sleep was difficult. I was the one that slept all night.

Combat soldiers averaged less than six hours of sleep. Add sleep deprivation, exposure to all kinds of weather, hard physical labor, and the tremendous stress of life in a combat zone worked to lower morale, reduce physical stamina, and often impaired judgment. Accounts of jumpy soldiers on guard duty were common. Sometimes the sound of the wind or a pounding rain made hearing an approaching enemy difficult. Even a veteran soldier who could control his imagination, felt emotionally drained after two hours of maintaining top alertness.[28] Several moonlit nights while on guard duty, I heard a scurrying sound within the bushes and yelled, "Halt," but nothing happened. To this day, I will never know whether or not I allowed a German patrol to get through our lines. Several nights a German breakthrough was feared, so half of the platoon stayed awake in shifts of four hours each.

Often, soldiering required us to improvise to get the job done. One time the first squad needed gravel to patch the shell holes on a road and the only place we found any gravel was on a railroad track between the ties. As we started shoveling gravel, we heard from some men who were repairing the track. Their leader ordered us to stop shoveling, so we put the gravel back and left with our collective tails between our legs.

On June 22nd, we were part of the attack on the outer defenses of Cherbourg carrying bangalore torpedoes to be used when we encountered barbed wire. The Air Corps was to make an attack on the planes and had asked us to mark the frontlines by displaying three-colored panels of

---

[28] Kindsvatter 33-34

chartreuse, cerise and white. Chartreuse and cerise colors were determined to be the best reflective colors. Fifty-five years later, emergency vehicles still use chartreuse and the army in Iraq still uses cerise panels on trucks to identify them from an attack by air. When the service company displayed the panels on the front lines that day, everybody below got strafed or bombed, so the panels were used only once.

That same afternoon while crossing a street in a small village, I was caught in the street as P-38's and Spitfires strafed the area. I hit the ground as bullets hit on both sides of me only inches away from my body. This was the first life of the cat's nine lives. I was amazed that we suffered no casualties from the misplaced bombs and machine gun fire.

Our platoon went into a field and took up positions behind the hedgerow when all hell broke loose. Mortars, rockets and artillery 88's pinned us down. The shells and rockets exploded in the trees so close to us that our bodies were thrown into the air about six to twelve inches. When the shelling stopped after an hour or so, I looked around and found myself alone. Everyone was gone. The squad had run away without my noticing. I don't remember much after that except around dusk (10 p.m.), I was with the command post of the 313th Infantry. When more shells came and officers ran to where I was behind a hedgerow, Col. Sterling Wood and Lt. Col. Van Bibber, flopped down not 20 feet from me. Beyond that, my memories of that day are gone. Next I found myself walking down a road at 1:30 p.m. I thought this is quite a celebration for my 20th birthday— no birthday cake—instead I was lost in a battle zone. A miracle occurred when I ran into Sgt. Jacobsen and four or five members of our platoon. We passed a burning truck hit by artillery, exploding and crackling, only to discover that the burning truck was our own supply truck, our equipment, and that the explosions were from a hundred pound box of TNT. We joined a few other members and set up a campsite. Before sleeping on the ground, I thanked God for taking care of me. I had used my second "cat's nine lives."

The next day the attack continued toward Cherbourg. Company A was called to blow a path through barbed wire with bangalore torpedoes. In the afternoon, the infantry came upon a deep anti-tank ditch twelve feet deep and fiffteen feet across. We brought up a D-6 bulldozer and, after dark, filled in the ditch allowing the troops and tanks to proceed. I don't remember his name, but I know that man was an expert with the dozer. The roar of the dozer engine draws artillery which makes it very dangerous work. We entered a building that the Germans had left only hours before as evidenced by the smell of Turkish tobacco, sour cooked cabbage, and old leather that permeated the room. We noticed these same odors when we came into buildings occupied by German soldiers.

Early in the afternoon, we noticed several hundred men kneeling in an orchard while three chaplains served communion and prayed for the men's safety.

SURVIVAL IN COMBAT: LESSONS FROM THE FIRST DAY

A well-trained mortar crew can get six shells in the air before the first one lands. Each successive shell lands fifteen to twenty feet further back since the natural reaction to being shelled is to run back; thereby running into the five remaining shells.

The first day mortars came in, my three companions ran and one was hit and wounded. One reason for my survival during 220 days of combat is that during almost every step I took in the combat zone, I asked myself where I would go if a shell came in. Since I knew where to go to get cover, I had the advantage.

Men in an infantry division are within range of artillery fire all the time. I learned to live with the possibility of death at any moment. Men who could not adjust to these living conditions were candidates for battle fatigue.

As told by Bernat Rosen and Frederick Tubach in *"An Uncommon Friendship—in a Thumbnail Sketch of a Survivor"*:

"Instincts for the smallest opportunities; mental toughness; the ability to roll with the punches; the ability to not be anguished by horrible sights; to insulate yourself from your surroundings when faced with unremitting horrors. The ability to become callous, to armor yourself, to hibernate, to slow your breathing nearly to a halt; you hunker down...to stick like a barnacle to a rock or under water crevice, to cling to your spot, unaffected while crashing waves rolled over you."

Most combat men could understand what this author went through in concentration camp.[29]

In the early days of the Normandy campaign, captured snipers confessed that they had accepted the position

---

[29] Rosen & Tubach

because they knew Americans did not shoot their prisoners. While it's true that the American army rarely shot prisoners, once under sniper fire, every GI in the area aimed for that sniper. In fact, the only time I fired my M-1 was at a sniper in an apple tree! [30]

In Normandy, the many fruit trees and their undergrowth in the hedgerows offered enemy snipers natural hiding places, and the Germans made the most of these opportunities. Snipers would hide in the branches of apple trees and shoot the GI's as they cleared the trees. After they ran out of ammunition, they jumped down and surrendered. Even though the rules of war outlawed killing them, soldiers often killed snipers as they would try to surrender. Soldiers detest snipers, and the Americans were no different, especially the high level officers.[31] As General Bradley's aide Major Hansen recorded:

> *"Talk of sniping and Bradley says he will not take action against anyone that decides to treat the snipers a little more roughly than they are being treated at present. Snipers cannot sit around and shoot and then be captured when you close in on them. That's not the way to play the game."* [32]

One day they gave us bottles of rum, cognac or wine. Most of us took only a drink or two. Willie Hunter, a rough and ready PFC from Virginia, drank a fifth of rum. He passed out and laid on the ground for ten hours. We walked around him, and let him recover on his own.

Our battalion chaplain, a Lutheran named Major Nordgren, held services on two Sundays. The first service, three or four attended and at the second only I attended. His service was ritual and prayers. No further services were scheduled until March 1945. (See Appendix on Chaplains.)

---

[30] Cross of Lorraine 3
[31] Carafano 50
[32] Hansen War Diary MHI

On the morning of June 26th, the 313th Regiment entered Cherbourg. The seacoast guns of Fort Du Roule fired large guns into the rear units all day. As they crossed the railroad track in their jeep, Captain Varnum, Sgt. Phelps and the driver were hit, killing them all. I thought of Capt. Varnum's pretty wife from the company ceremony in Camp Phillips, Kansas. The city was wild with soldiers roaming the city carrying bottles of booze in their shirts. The 79th Division captured the commissary, taking thirteen truckloads of liquor and wine. Liquor was typically distributed only during the year on Christmas, New Year's Day, etc.

Left without commanders, about fifteen of us gathered in town and discussed what to do. I suggested to Lt. Warga that we move outside of the city where it was less dangerous. He agreed and we jumped on jeeps. From being the lowest ranking member of Company A, I was suddenly now among the leaders. The jeep I was on carried thirteen of us. We camped in an apple orchard for the night. On June 27th we moved south to be a part of the VIII Corps. The division rested and received replacements for a week before going back into the front line.

Life in the Normandy hedgerows continued to be an adventure. The windshields had to be turned down or taken away and placed on the hoods of cars or trucks due to light reflecting on them. The Germans would string a cable across the road and the jeep drivers would not see the cable and be decapitated. To counter this threat, steel rods were welded onto the radiator.

After three days of combat, I saw a soldier taking five or six prisoners to the rear. He fired stones at them to get them to run and then shot all of them. He told me they were running away, so he shot them. He was angry at seeing so many of his buddies killed or wounded. On top of that, he knew his unit was very short-handed and even more so while he was taking prisoners to the rear area. Culture is a thin veneer and limits of human endurance are reached quickly under extreme circumstances (See Appendix—Battle Fatigue)

One day the third platoon was given the job of fixing beach cottages on the English Channel. We would sweep for booby traps and make sure everything was working. I enjoyed the day at the beach and couldn't help wondering what the owners were like. I also thought that, if not for the war, I would be at Ottertail Lake in Minnesota. These cottages were to be used as rest areas for battle fatigue soldiers. Whether these cottages were ever used in this manner, we will never know.

Mail call was held infrequently under combat conditions, but when the mail finally came, it was truly a special occasion. Combat men thought mail provided the major connection to that far-away world. Soldiers spoke of the memories of home that the mail provided. Mail call was a special event for a GI. It provided several minutes for him to withdraw into his private world. Packages helped the GI cope with the violent world. Food, clothing and other useful items from home made life at the front a little easier.[33]

In July or August 1944 the army started the V-mail program to reduce the thousands of sacks of mail each day to the troops overseas. The correspondents in the states wrote on a special V-mail form that was made into microfilm. The microfilm containing thousands of letters was mailed and then the film was printed into letter form and sent to the proper soldiers.

The wives of two soldiers in my platoon had a unique way of staying in touch with their husbands. These women snipped off their pubic hair and sent it to their husbands through the

---

[33] Kindsvatter 109

mail, as a remembrance of happier days. The married men that received these pink-ribboned packages would carry them in their billfolds. When they would take them out, they would get teary-eyed as they cast their minds back to their days of married life. These remembrance packages may have been effective in keeping the men faithful to their wives, as the men who received these packages did not run around with women in England or France.

On the day that Cherbourg fell, our squad entered a bar in that town. Several of us went into the restroom, where we encountered an atrocious sight: there was a urinal, but instead of a toilet, we found two raised steps and a hole into which we would have had to do our business. The place was such a mess that no one used it.

8

Normandy—Hedgerows

The battle line faced south and stretched about sixty miles, from Caen on the east to La Haye-Du-Puits and the ocean on the west. The First Army was made up of three corps—from V, VII, and VIII on the left to right with nine divisions in the line.

On July 3rd, 1944, the 79th Division joined the VIII Corps commanded by Major General Troy H. Middleton with the 79th, 82nd Airborne, and 90th Division near the La Haye-Du-Puits and Montgarden. Our positions were on extreme right on the Atlantic Ocean.

Hedgerows in Normandy

The American Command was concerned by the slow progress in the VIII Corps area. Much of the slow progress was due to the weather. Normandy had its wettest July in over 40 years. One bombing unit of marauders had seventeen straight missions scrubbed in the first 2½ weeks in July. More than any other factor, this weather explains the relative German success in Normandy in July 1944. Rain and fog allowed them to move reinforcements and supplies to the front lines.[34]

The 749th Tank Battalion, the 813th Tank Destroyer Battalion and the 463rd Division Anti-aircraft Battalion were attached to the 79th Division. The 79th Division jumped off at 5:30 a.m. on July 3rd, after a 15-minute artillery preparation. The area from the ocean to La Haye-Du-Puits had the extreme right of VIII Corps front, with the 82nd Airborne in the middle and the 90th on the left. The 79th Division assignment was to assault the Montgarden Ridge and Hill 121 west of La Haye-Du-Puits.

The next ten days were an ordeal fought in the worst hedgerows in Normandy. Interestingly, these hedgerows are the only remaining hedgerows in Normandy. The rain hindered the attack of July 3rd and continued into July 4th. At noon on July 4th, every artillery piece fired a salvo at the German positions on the order of the Commanding General Bradley.

The German positions commanded the high ground, close in areas were swept by machine guns leaving no dead spots. The intermediate areas were covered by mortars and by flanking fire from batteries of 170mm guns and high velocity weapons. My memory of the next five days is filled with sad thoughts of artillery, mortars, constant machine gun and rifle fire and jeeps fitted out as ambulances with men on stretchers.[35] Russell Weigley stated, "The artillery was the outstanding combat

[34] Ambrose, Citizen Soldiers 66
[35] 313th History 82

branch of the American ground forces." The Americans were able to use the artillery of an entire corps (about 200 guns) on a target, sometimes called a *"Serenade"* and sometimes a *"Time on Target (TOT)"* by calculating the trajectory of each shell so that every shell hit at the same time. Survivors of a TOT serenade were witnesses to the horrible effects.[36]

The Germans had nothing to compare with our 155 MM long toms, considered the best in long-range artillery. We had twelve per division and many more for each corps.

The battle for the high ground at Montgarden was fought in an almost continuous manner from July 3rd to July 15th. At the end on July 15th, the 313th Infantry had lost so many men that they were no longer a fighting unit. Some companies had lost 70% of their men. The 313th Regiment withdrew for six days to regroup with replacements of men and equipment.

Our squad was ordered to blow up mines on a road. Six of us were busy binding two sticks of TNT together and attaching primer cord and a fuse. I didn't notice the five squad members leaving, but I noticed they were gone when I suddenly heard five shells exploding. I had a strange premonition that a guardian angel had kept me safe. When they got back, the men reported the Germans had direct fire on the road. When they heard the incoming shells, they jumped into five of the six holes at hand. The sixth hole, the one I would have occupied, received a direct hit! This was number three of the cat's nine lives!

David Frazer's Knights Cross describes the battle in the Hedgerows from the German perspective.

> *"American progress in the continent was relentless, in*
> *Bocage, the close hedgerow country in the center of the front,*

---

[36] Larrabee 469

there was an unending sequence of enemy pushes, both small scale and large scale, each accompanied by intensive artillery and air attack. This was fighting of a particularly expensive kind, high in casualties, small advances purchased with a good deal of blood, both of attackers and defenders."[37]

Tactically, the men of Army Group B still felt they often had the best of it, but their strength was being sapped by attrition. The front was long—two million men were contesting it. Rommel still got a good impression of the fighting troops on his visits, but he knew they were suffering.

The Americans had twelve divisions in the field, but their main advantage was their ability to call on virtually unlimited reinforcements of men, equipment, and supplies while at the same time the German army was wasting away. Rommel reported the army had lost 117,000 men including 2700 officers from June 6 to July 15 and had received ten thousand replacements.[38]

During late June and early July, the First Army tried to solve the tactical and technical problems in the Bocage. In early July, Company A was issued a Sherman tank with a dozer blade attached. Sgt. Smith was the tank commander. They opened a path through several hedgerows for the infantry to charge through. The sounds of the tank cutting into the hedgerows drew artillery fire. For his daring accomplishment, Sgt. Smith was awarded a Silver Star and received a battlefield appointment to 2nd Lt. Later in July, the First Army perfected the technique of penetrating the hedgerows. Several hundred Sherman tanks were fitted in front with steel blades fashioned from the steel obstacles on Omaha Beach. They formed attack teams of one Rhino tank, a combat engineer team, riflemen and a 60mm

[37] Fraser 501
[38] Fraser 501

mortar. The Sherman started the attack by plowing its blade through the hedgerow, then firing white phosphorus shells in the corners of the next hedgerow from its 75mm cannon. This knocked out the German dug-in machine gun pits. After firing the white phosphorus shells, the Sherman fired 50-caliber machine guns along the base of opposite hedgerows. The mortar group lobbed mortars into the field. The infantry squad ran behind the tank and advanced across the field closer to the enemy's hedgerow, then lobbed hand grenades over the hedgerow.[39]

ARMY AIR CORPS

American air superiority was decisive in Normandy. The ground units had to call England for permission and directions. The use of panels, or smoke, was proven ineffective.

The solution to the problem came from Major General Elwood Quesada of the 9th Tactical Air Force in England. The slowness of the advance and the thousands of casualties convinced him that the 9th Air Force fighter bombers had to make a greater contribution to the conflict. He joined Bradley to explore new methods. For example, artillery units have forward observers who pass on target information by radio or telephone to the gunners. He suggested to Bradley that we equip the fighter/bombers and artillery units with UHF radios so they can spot and talk to each other. Bradley agreed, they tried it, and it worked to near perfection. The next suggestion was to equip Sherman tanks with radios as well. This new system worked so well that the P-47's were able to bomb targets within 500 meters of the front lines. P-47's carried the air power with an awesome display of weaponry: two five-inch by four-foot

---

[39] Ambrose, Citizen Solders 67,68

missiles under each wing, plus two 500-pound bombs in addition to 6,400 rounds of 50-caliber machine gun ammo.

As described by David Fraser in Knight's Cross, the German troops were in a very critical situation:

> *"Our soldiers, wrote one of Rommel's Commanders, enter the battle in low spirits at the thought of the enemy's enormous material superiority. They were asking where is the Luftwaffe? The feeling of helplessness against enemy aircraft without any hindrance has a paralyzing effect and during the barrage. This effect on inexperienced troops is literally soul shaking, and losses were appalling from artillery as well as air strikes. Even the smallest enemy attacks appeared to be preceded by saturation bombardment. On 14 July, Rommel found one parachute regiment with a total of one thousand reinforcements received since the battle began, over eight hundred had already fallen. The morale was good, The Chief of Staff of Panzer Troup West told Rommel "But we can't beat the materiel of the enemy with courage alone."*[40]

The history of the 313th Infantry Regiment describes the horrors of the Battle of Montgarden and the Normandy Campaign as follows:

> *"There can be no question about the fighting at Montgarden and for that matter, during the entire period of the Normandy Campaign, represented the most difficult and the most hazardous combat that the 313th Infantry had yet experienced.... in the first place the troops were fresh when the battle for Cherbourg began. They were ready, almost eager, for the adventure ahead. Now they were tired and battle weary. They were bucking, day in and day out, the*

---

[40] Fraser 506

nightmarish hell of the hedgerows, where every field was a death trap and progress was reckoned in terms of yards not miles. Throughout all of the Normandy countryside, the enemy was well dug in, and he lay in waiting well concealed, prepared for almost perfect defensive warfare. At Montgarden the enemy positions for defense were so sited that every avenue of approach was well-covered by all types of enemy fire. All efforts to skirt or surround enemy resistance met with little success, and the only formula which would or could work was that of weeding the enemy out hedgerow by hedgerow. To do this, losses were necessarily high, and many times the morale of the men almost reached the breaking point, but always they carried on, undaunted by initial failures, and finally succeeded in driving the enemy back."[41]

An article in World War II magazine describes the condition of the men after extended combat:

"The New Zealanders relieved the 34th Division, whose battle-scarred veterans did not say much, but their gaunt, hollow-eyed faces were a mute but eloquent testimony to their lengthy ordeal, an eyewitness remembered. "It was more than the stubble of beard that told the story: it was the blank staring eyes. The men were so tired that it was like a living death." [42]

(The 34th Division, the Minnesota, North Dakota national, had soldiers from my hometown as well as my brother-in-law's.)

Fatigue, fear and stress were the cause of "psychic numbing." In its extreme form, it is best summed up by the description of what World War II soldiers called the thousand-yard stare. The infantry soldiers were in a bad way as described by Ernie Pyle:

---

[41] History of the 313th 83
[42] World War II magazine, July 2003 "Eric Niderost— Quest for the Eternal City" 38-44

"It's a look of dullness, eyes that look without seeing, eyes that see without conveying any image to the mind. It's a look that shows—exhaustion, lack of sleep, tension for too long, weariness that is too great, fear beyond fear, misery to the point of numbness, a look of surpassing indifference to anything anybody can do. It's a look I dread to see on men."[43]

Soldiers and psychiatrists came to understand that "every man had his breaking point." You can hear just so many shells, see just so many torn bodies, fear just so much fear, soak just so much rain, and spend just so many sleepless nights.[44]

Ernie Pyle stated casualties were bearable to the GI only when there were not too many or too often. "It's when casualties become so great that those who remain feel they have no chance to live if they have to go on and on taking it—that's when morale in an army gets low."[45]

Men of the 79th Division had many of these feelings during the intense battles in Alsace. The infantrymen who entered combat on June 18, 1944 believed "it can't happen to me," then "it CAN happen to me," then "it WILL happen to me."

After a three-day attack, the 79th Division broke the German lines on July 14 forcing a withdrawal to the Ay River south of Lessday. The front remained inactive until COBRA on July 26th, the 79th, still with the VIII Corps.

After the battle for high ground at Montgarden, also known as The Bloody Hill, some of us climbed to the top of Montgarden. We were amazed how everything below could be seen, and immediately understood how the Germans had been able to shell every move we made.

---

[43] Pyle, Brave Men 270
[44] Martin 339
[45] Pyle, Brave Men 103

On July 14th, Bastille Day, A Company was selected to form the honor guard for the celebration in La Haye-Du-Puits. The Mayor, in formal dress with numerous medals on his chest, made a speech thanking us for liberating the city. We also got a kiss on both cheeks.

BATTLEFIELD COMMUNICATIONS

Each infantry company was equipped with a radio and a soldier assigned to carry the heavy transmitter. Radios were used with caution since the German equipment was able to determine our location through radio transmissions. Often, radio resulted in artillery or mortar shelling. Each unit laid telephone lines to their regiment or division, resulting in numerous wires strung alongside the roads. These wires had to be lifted up on poles at every intersection. Artillery and tanks often caused breaks in lines. German patrols would cut lines then re-tape them leaving a gap in the line. We often saw a Signal Corps man following his line, looking for a break.

COST OF THE BATTLE FOR NORMANDY

Near La Haye-Du-Puits in the twelve days prior to July 14th, the VIII Corps had over 10,000 casualties and had moved less than eight miles. In the 79th Division, a typical rifle company had one officer and only forty-seven men on July 10th.

Battle fatigue was an ongoing problem. A Company had a good number of cases of battle fatigue. My squad of thirteen men had three cases of battle fatigue—a sergeant, a corporal, and a PFC. Each man approached me with their inability to adjust to the shelling and seeing their friends wounded or killed. The NCOs were the ones who bragged about leading us into combat. My words of comfort seemed to help. The PFC, a burly coal miner from Pennsylvania, was critically wounded in a mortar attack. We had only one more case of battle fatigue for the war during our experience in a Lorraine foxhole filled with water.

The 304th Engineers were tasked with checking for mines and removing any mines that were discovered. I have little memory of the days before the breakout. One moonlight night, I found myself looking for food in an abandoned foxhole. I remember thinking that it is 1:30 a.m. and I hadn't eaten since breakfast. This indicated the high level of despair in those days described above, since I have an almost photographic memory of the events of 1944-45.

One historian observed that few Europeans and Americans of the post-war generation grasped just how intense the early Overlord battles were in the demands they made upon the foot soldier who came closer than any other in the west in the second world war to match the horror of the eastern front or of Flanders war years earlier. Many...infantry units suffered over 100 percent casualties..."[46]

The 79th Division suffered 2,930 casualties in eleven days' fighting from July 4-15. This is very high considering that the three infantry regiments had a total of 9,000 men.

The battle in the hedgerows ended with a terrible cost, The Army's official history states:

> *"Heroic exertion seemed on the surface to have accomplished little—with twelve divisions, the First Army in seventeen days had advanced only about seven miles in the area west of the Vire and little more than half that distance east of the River—to reach positions along the Lessay-*

46 Hastings 12

Caumont line, the First Army had sustained approximately 40,000 casualties during July, of which 90% were infantrymen...The majority of the casualties were caused by shell fragments involving in many cases multiple wounds. Many other men suffered combat fatigue, not always counted in the casualty reports, they nevertheless totaled an additional twenty-five to thirty-three percent of the number of men physically wounded...We won the battle of Normandy, one survivor later said, (BUT) considering the high price of American lives we LOST." Not a bitter indictment of the way warfare was conducted in the Hedgerows, the statement revealed instead the feeling of despair that touched all who participated." [47]

79th Division
at La Haye-Du-Puits

Memorial at
La Haye-Du-Puits

---

[47] Blumerson 175-176

9

Normandy Breakout

As July 1944 came to an end, the war was a stalemate with progress marked by yards instead of miles. General Bradley finally concentrated on an all-out air attack, named COBRA.

Prior to the attack, American troops were withdrawn 1,500 yards. Bradley concentrated the bombing on a narrow 7,000-yard front in the VII Corps Area. Bradley requested the bombers make their runs parallel to the front. His request was refused by airmen who insisted the attacks should be perpendicular to U.S. lines. Eyewitness accounts, as well as my own memories, describe this earth-shattering event:

> *"July 25th dawned a clear day. At 9:38 a.m., 550 fighter-bombers, mostly P-47's, fired rockets and machine guns, dropped 500-pound bombs that could be dropped by the pilots within 300 meters of the American lines. After the attack by P-47's, 1800 B-17s came over. Their appearance was so astounding that words could hardly express its reality. Ernie Pyle described it as follows: "A new sound gradually droned into our ears; a gigantic far-away surge of doom like sound, it was the heavies. They came from directly behind us; they came in flights of twelve, three flights to a group and in groups stretched out across the sky. Their march across the sky was slow and studied."* [48]

[48] Murray & Millett 428

Gen. Fritz Bayerlein of the Panzer Lehr Division compared the flight to a conveyor belt. My memory coincides with Ernie Pyle's. It was an awesome sight to see 1,800 B-17's flying at 10,000 feet coming on and on for over sixty minutes. I marveled at the fact that the U.S. in January of 1942 had almost no airpower and $2\frac{1}{2}$ years later could display almost 3,000 planes in one operation. Most of the men in our squad could hardly believe their eyes and ears. I mentioned to my friend, Oldham, this event will never be repeated in our lifetime.

The B-17's bombs saturated the area south of the road to a distance of 2,500 meters. The damage done to the Germans was catastrophic. Reports of witnesses described the bombed area as looking like the surface of the moon. It was difficult to identify craters because they overlapped. The blasts wiped out entire hedgerows.[49]

"General Bayerlein reported the loss of at least 70% of his troops, out of action, dead, wounded, crazed, or numbed"[50]

"After the B-17's ended their runs, about 350 P-47's came in for another twenty-minute attack. The P-47's dropped napalm bombs on the target as the infantry and tanks were ready to advance; 400 B-26's hit the rear of the German front lines."[51]

The decision to bomb perpendicular to the front lines had terrible consequences on July 24. Bad weather cancelled the bombing. A number of planes did not get the information so bombed anyway, with many of the bombs falling short on U.S. troops, killing 25 Americans and wounding 131 men.

On July 25, errors by the B-17's as the smoke bombs drifted resulted in a large bombardment on American positions. These

---

[49] Tobin 332
[50] Hastings 256
[51] Overy 208

misdirected bombs killed 111 Americans, including Lt. Gen. Leslie McNair and 490 soldiers were wounded. While the bombardment did not entirely break the enemy's will to resist, it hurt the Germans badly.[52]

REORGANIZATION

Setting up the 12th Army Group under Bradley:

1st Army - Hodges
3rd Army - Patton

The First Army had grown unwieldy. It consisted of three corps, V, VII, VIII and fifteen divisions in the line and an infantry and an armored division to land shortly. One army headquarters could no longer maintain satisfactory control. The problem would be compounded when there would be fourteen infantry, six armored, and two airborne divisions expected to be in the ETO by July 1944 and four more divisions expected by August. By July 29th there were almost a million American soldiers in France. There also were 600,000 British and almost 900,000 tons of supplies and 176,620 vehicles and 156,025 vehicles for the British.[53]

After the July 25th bombing on the VII Corps front, the 4th, 9th and 30th Divisions moved into the moon-like landscape the bombers had created.

---

[52] Murray & Millett 428 - 429
[53] Weigley 170

They experienced a strong resistance by the remaining German troops. The 1st and 2nd Armored Divisions joined the fight and made a fifteen mile advance from lines of July 25th, 1944.

On the VIII Corps front, the 79th Division had cleared the Bocage and occupied the high ground overlooking the Ay river north of Lessay. The plan called for the 79th Division, along side the 8th Division, to cross the Ay river. Hidden minefields were discovered and quickly cleared by Company A of the 304th Engineers Battalion. (The author is in the picture on the previous page, taken from the 79th Division book.) On the 28th, the division pushed on another twelve–fourteen kilometers against light resistance.[54]

PATTON'S THIRD ARMY

The Third Army was an army of movement. It was the only fully mechanized army created for the purpose of maneuver speed and exploitation. Indeed, the Third Army and its general were literally made for each other.

"General Patton was given the command of the Third Army because of his audacity, boldness, and ruthlessness, not in spite of it. In turn, the Third Army had been created specifically as a mobile force, using its twentieth century technology to apply the cavalry concept to seek out, disrupt, and destroy the enemy. It was soldiers such as Generals Patton, Harmon, Walker, and dozens more who were cavalrymen first and tank generals second. They used the tried-and-true...cavalry methods in conjunction with their new fire-belching iron horses to create a type of warfare that surpasses even the best applications of the Germans. These cavalrymen are the ones who took the concept of blitzkrieg (lightning war) and made it into an art form."[55]

[54] History of the 79th 36
[55] Province 291

The American army had been fighting the U.S. Grant model-infantry attacks on a broad front with COBRA. Now they were back to the Cavalry / General Custer model of open country attacks by armored divisions and infantry divisions who switched roles, following up the armored spearheads and mopping up scattered enemy units located in towns.

The 79th Division, part of VIII Corps, was in the Third Army under George Patton, who inspired everyone working under him to a greater level of performance. The 313th Infantry was motorized and made part of Combat Command B of the 6th Armored. Company A was also a part of the 6th Armored column. The mission was to take and secure Granville, twenty miles down the road. Once the mission was accomplished, we were on the road again.

The army provided 400 trucks, holding 10,000 troops, so that the infantry could move as fast as the armored divisions. The sight of thousands of vehicles of every type and make—jeeps, trucks, artillery, huge trucks—filling every east-bound road was truly awesome.

The breakout provided the first breath of air since June 7; the hedgerows of death and destruction lay behind us. Everyone was jubilant because we were rolling miles each day, instead of yards. The infantrymen were now clean-shaven and no longer had an exhausted look, which made them appear fully five years younger.

We spent the next few days in our truck as part of a never-ending convoy. The line of trucks would roll a mile or two and then stop for an hour or two. Several times there was a call for the BARMAN (Browning Automatic Rifleman). He came and in a few minutes, we heard gunfire against snipers. Once the 105mm guns fired at a church steeple to kill observers and snipers. Unfortunately, many churches had their steeples destroyed in this manner.

On August 2nd, after a long convoy ride, we passed through Avranches, which sits on great bluffs overlooking the Bay of St. Michel. When camped near the Pontaubault Bridge, it was the first night that we did not dig a slit trench for security against shelling. Just after dark, German Stukkas started to bomb the bridge. The Stukka dive bombers attacked with a shrieking siren noise. I dove under the lumber trailer as the explosions seemed very close and the anti-aircraft artillery was also very loud, with shrapnel falling nearby. The attacks finally ended, allowing us to get three hours of sleep. The next morning, we crossed the bridge, barrage balloons protected the bridge. No damage to the bridge, but bomb-craters were in plain view of the bridge.

THE COASTAL TOWN

The 4th Armored Division captured the coastal town of Avranches, the key exit point from Normandy, after an advance of twenty-five miles over a thirty-six hour period. Its crucial achievement was to have seized intact the bridge at Pontubault, which carried the road from Avranches, southward across the river Selune. It provided the only ready route toward the objectives Bradley had given Patton's orders to send senior officers out to the feeder routes which led to it with orders to keep the vehicles rolling without regard for strict sequence of units. At the other end the bunched columns were scrambled by the simple means of marking each of the roads which fanned from it for a separate division. In this way, which defied every rule of Army Staff College logistics, his twelve divisions were gotten into the new theatre of operation in seventy-two hours.[56] (Figuring 15,000 men per division for a total of over 175,000 men and 50,000 vehicles.)[57]

---

[56] Keegan 237
[57] Murray & Millett 463

After crossing the bridge, officers, including colonels and MP's, directed each division's vehicles to their designated route. No straggling or delays were tolerated. The sight of thousands of vehicles of every description was almost beyond our comprehension. We could see columns of traffic on every road going east. Some of the dirt and gravel roads produced a cloud of dust. Two armored divisions turned west to capture the port cities of Brittany. This decision to attack Brittany was one of the war's bad decisions, since the four- or eight-week delay meant we were one corps short in the drive across France.

AMERICAN AIRPOWER

The U.S. Air Corps played an essential role in breaking the pockets of German resistance that delayed Patton's advancing columns. Major General Elwood "Pete" Quesada, of the XIX Tactical Air Command was one of the most involved leaders. He suggested putting pilots with radios in the leading armored vehicles as forward air controllers. In that way, Quesada could provide advancing American troops with effective air support as needed. US fighter bombers played an essential part in breaking up pockets of enemy resistance, which permitted Patton's advancing columns to maintain their speedy advance.[58]

In a documentary film of the U.S. air attacks, some German troops were wishing they could go to the Russian front where they wouldn't be hunted down from the sky by hundreds of Jabos (the German word for American fighter planes). American fighter-bombers patrolled the sky, shooting up and bombing anything that moved in the German rear areas. The evidence of their overall effectiveness was seen in demolished vehicles, roads, and railroads. Ground troops in 1944-45 will never forget

---

[58] Murray & Millett 431

the sight of over a thousand heavy bombers going over at 20,000 feet with a thousand exhaust trails lighting up the sky. We could often not see the planes, only their trails were visible. This sight almost certainly intimidated the Germans on the ground.

On August 3rd, General Bradley assigned the 79th Division to the XV Corps, telling General Patton, "For Christ's sake what are you doing with this open flank you have. I've sent the 79th down there, and I hate to bypass a commander, it's your Army." According to his diary, his reply was something about "Bradley's getting a British complex of over-caution." But otherwise Patton took Bradley's intervention in stride. He was exhilarated to be back in the field and was determined not to risk his position.[59]

The 79th's mission was to protect the open flank between the First Army and the Mayenne River to Fougereres. General Patton also assigned the 5th Armored Division and the 90th Division to the same area.

The 79th captured Fougereres on August 4th, and on August 6th moved east across the Mayene River to Laval. The 90th Division was on the right and the 5th Armored in the middle. The 79th Division encountered many road blocks in its drive toward Laval, but reached the Mayene River at 1600 on August 6th to find the bridges blown and the infantry crossed on a dam. A foot bridge was put in below the dam, and Company A placed treads on boats to ferry troops and vehicles across. By 1830, Company B completed a treadway bridge, which the 313th used to cross vehicles and antitank guns. A floating Bailey bridge arrived and was completed by Company C, 304th Division by noon.[60]

---

[59] Weigley 183
[60] Weigley 190

The XV Corps was given orders to continue advancing on August 7th on LeMans. The 90th was on the left, the 79th in the center and the 5th Armored on the right. Company A was attached to the 313th Infantry, with the 749 Tank Battalion, the 813th Tank Destroyer battalion, two battalions of artillery, the 79th Reconnaissance Troop, and a medical company making up the task force. The 106th Cavalry Group and the 79th Reconnaissance Group spearheaded the advance.[61]

The days of August 8-11 were spent in one long convoy of vehicles of every kind, moving east through dozens of small towns until we reached LeMans.

The history of the 313th Infantry states,

"The entire period was one of sharp contrasts. It was a period of bitter combat at one moment and the next moment the scene would shift to that of a triumphant procession of allied men and equipment through town after town, with newly liberated Frenchmen cheering wildly as the column moved along. It was a period when impossible and the unexpected were commonplace—all along the route of march the average French citizen seemed to react similarly. The moments when the Americans arrived, a spark was kindled that in mere matter of the moments reached a frenzied fire. Frenchmen appeared from nowhere, oblivious of the danger of life and limb, to cheer the advancing column on their way." [62]

These days in a convoy of tanks and trucks were a very enjoyable experience, with everyone's morale sky-high when contrasted to the terrible time in the hedgerows only days before. We were all looking for the war to be over before the snow came. Each evening we watched the sun sink in a ball of

---

[61] History of the 313th 91
[62] History of the 313th 91

orange color (dust particles in the air caused the orange glow). It was a peaceful scene in rural France, which reminded me of the painting of the Angelus. The French peasants harvested wheat or oats with horse drawn binders. Seeing shocks of wheat brought back memories of the harvest fields in the Red River Valley in Minnesota. The war seemed far away as the nights passed by with almost complete silence. "Bedcheck Charlie" was the only reminder of the war.

Many thousands of German prisoners were captured. They were forced into long flatbed trucks. When a truck appeared full, it would roll forward and suddenly stop, forcing the men to compress tighter into the truck bed, then the army would cram a dozen more prisoners into the truck. These overloaded trucks were very unstable and the human load would shift as the truck turned from side to side. The load of men was comparable to a load of hogs going to market. We noticed a number of these trucks in the ditch with the POW's scrambling to get back on the truck.

ALENCON – FALAISE GAP

After taking LeMans, the XV Corps was to drive north, the 2nd French Armored Division on the left and the 5th Armored on the right, followed by the 79th to move through Manners to Sees.

The 2nd French Armored Division, followed by the 90th Division, was to move to the road junction of Alencon.[63] The 314th was motorized to follow the 5th Armored; the 313th and 315th after a nineteen-mile march came into positions. The evening of August 12, the XV Corps was in Alencon and seemed ready to drive north with four divisions to close the lower

---

[63] Weigley 201

portion of the eighteen miles wide gap. General Patton thought it unlikely that the Canadians would close the gap quickly so ordered the XV Corps to push on toward Falaise to close the gap.

When General Bradley heard of Patton's order, he ordered Patton not to proceed north of Argenton, which was one of the most controversial decisions of the campaign.[64] The only action the 79th saw happened on August 14th was when some German units tried to come through the division's positions.

The German army faced disaster at Falaise. General Montgomery thought the Canadians could reach Argentan from the north faster than the Americans from the south. Montgomery ordered the Canadians to proceed to capture Falaise and then go on to the Argentan.

General Bradley reluctantly agreed to hold the XV Corps at Argentan. The British and the Canadian army were known at the time for caution and failure. To reach objectives in a timely manner at the same time, they repeatedly failed to perceive the ability of the American army to move rapidly and decisively under conditions of mobile warfare. [65]

These delays in closing the pocket from August 13th through 20th, 1944, aided the Germans in getting out 20,000 to 40,000 of the 100,0000 soldiers caught in the pocket. These included some of the toughest soldiers who were expected to provide the framework in rebuilding the German army in the west. Admittedly, they had lost most of their equipment, but back in Germany, Albert Speer's factories were producing huge amounts of armaments of all kinds to re-equip the small formation that escaped from Normandy.[66]

---

[64] D'Este 529-430
[65] D'Este 428
[66] Murray & Millett 432

The battle for Normandy destroyed what was left of the Germen mechanized army. The 7th and 15th Army relied on 670,000 horses for hauling artillery and supply vehicles. There were more than 14,500 trucks in Normandy that were restricted by a severe shortage of fuel and tires. From 2,300 tanks only 100 survived.[67]

In addition to the loss of vehicles, thousand of soldiers surrendered each day for a total of 50,000 men in all. The devastation caused inside the pocket from artillery and fighter-bombers was awesome, resulting in 10,000 German dead. "One American officer compared this with World War I, an avenging angel had swept the area bent on destroying all things German."[68]

General Eisenhower wrote:

> *"The battlefield at Falaise was unquestionably one of the greatest killing fields of any of the war areas. Roads, highways were so choked with destroyed equipment and dead men and animals that passage through was extremely difficult. Forty-eight hours after closing the Gap, I was conducted through it on foot, to encounter what could only be described by Dante. It was literally possible to walk for hundreds of yards at a time, stepping on nothing but dead and decaying flesh."* [69]

After the battle to close the Falaise gap, Company A was selected to help in the clean-up of a road near Falaise. Our task was to remove hundreds of dead horses that had been dead for five or more days. The problem was to place the winch cable under the horse without getting guts and blood all over. Since we didn't have gas masks, we covered our noses with handkerchiefs. The smell was overwhelming, but we survived.

---

[67] Overy 327
[68] Larabee 467
[68] Bradley 304

Three of our men discovered a destroyed German payroll truck. They came away with thousands of French francs. In an effort not to be detected, these men gave us bills to try to break up thousand of francs in serial order.

The U.S. had two armies of twenty divisions (600,000) and 3,000 tanks. Additionally, the US Air Corps had 12,000 planes. Both German armies had been destroyed in their effectiveness. From 10,000 to 15,000 in the Mortain-Falaise conflict, along with another 50,000 men were prisoners. The Germans had experienced almost 500,000 casualties in France since D-Day. The victory had been costly to the U.S., killed, wounded or missing, two thirds of them American

Returning to Normandy for the 50th Anniversary in 1999, my most thoughtful moment occurred when visiting the German cemetery in Normandy. The U.S. cemetery near Omaha Beach was picturesque—white crosses and green landscape with the Channel in the background. When viewing the graves of comrades from the 79th Division, I had an almost peaceful feeling thinking about their lives of sacrifice.

In sharp contrast stood the German cemetery. I walked among row after row of dark, almost black tombstones of soldiers who gave their lives in a war to satisfy Hitler's lust for power. There were no other visitors than our group, but I was alone with the memory of the hundreds of German dead that I had seen in Normandy and elsewhere. I couldn't help thinking, "Is there no one to mourn the thousands of soldiers sleeping in the German cemetery?"

10

The Seine River to Belgium

hen General Patton received Bradley's order stopping the XV Corps at Argenton, he alerted the 79th on August 14th for a trip east to Versailles and Paris. The division was to be motorized to advance behind the 106th Cavalry group and the French 2nd Armored Division. We started on the road to Chartres but on August 15th the mission of the division was changed to that of capturing the heights overlooking the Seine at Mantes-Gassicourt. The 4th and 29th D-Day Divisions were selected to enter Paris with the French 2nd Armored Division.

The division stayed near Nogent-le-Roi for several days. The division captured a German warehouse containing tons of grain, canned meat and other supplies, along with a German airport containing a large workshop and six partially intact planes. On August 16th, our entire division area was strafed by waves of German aircraft. Fifteen planes were shot down by anti-aircraft artillery, .30 caliber and .50 caliber small arms fire.[70]

When German planes flew over our positions, we fired M-1s and .30 and .50 caliber machine guns from the trucks. I was sitting on a crate eating lunch when a large piece of shrapnel from a 40mm Bofors gun hit the crate less than a foot from me. Another of the cat's nine lives was lost, but I survived.

---

[70] History of the 313th 93

The pre-planning of the invasion called for a pause at the Seine River to give the combat troops time for rest and replacement to bring the divisions up to strength. The main reason was to re-supply the army since everything was offloaded over the beaches, which were 100 miles away.

Bradley: A General Life states: "... with the enemy reeling in defeat, the planned pause at the Seine was clearly inappropriate. Regardless of the logistical limitations, which were growing ever more binding, we would, as Ike put it, to Marshall on August 17th, ' dash across the Seine without pause, both to prevent the Germans from creating defensive positions on the east bank and to entrap as many stragglers as possible in the north. Haislip XV Corps was already across the Seine at Mantes."[71]

On August 18th, the division was motorized to proceed to Mantes-Gassicourt, with the 313th on the left and the 314th on the right, while the 315th was left behind at Nogent-le-Roi to guard the bridges until relieved by the 5th Division. On August 19th, after an hour-long artillery barrage, the 314th drove into Mantes-Gassicourt, while the 313th approached the Seine and found a catwalk over the dam intact.

General Wyche received an order from General Patton at 9:35 p.m. to cross the Seine that very night. The 313th crossed over the catwalk in the dark and in a pouring rain, with each man clutching the man in front of him.

The next day, Company A, 304th Engineers ferried the 314th over the Seine in assault boats and rafts. My group

---

[71] Bradley 308

pulled a cable across the river about 200 meters long. We placed treads over three assault boats long enough to hold three jeeps, then three or four of us pulled on the cable to float the raft across. It was very difficult to pull the raft upstream. By 6:35 p.m. the operation was complete.

The Corps of Engineers had a treadway bridge ready and the 315th crossed on trucks, tanks, artillery, and heavy equipment followed. The Luftwaffe tried to knock out the bridge. Anti-aircraft guns destroyed twelve planes the first day and fifty in four days.[72]

The bridgehead was enlarged to nine kilometers on the first day. The division extended the bridgehead with three regiments abreast without incident. On securing the Seine bridgehead, the division remained in a defensive position for the next nine days. Ten additional batteries of corps artillery were brought up.

From August 22nd–25th the Germans counter-attacked in great force to wipe out the bridgehead. Thirty batteries of artillery fired 4,600 rounds of 105mm ammunition and 1,048 rounds of 155mm ammunition to stop these attacks.

On August 22nd, the 313th captured La Roche-Guyon, which had served as General Rommel's headquarters. The chateau was in perfect condition, with the air conditioning and the lights still working. This was the first place with electricity we had encountered since Charbourg. During our 50th D-day anniversary trip, the bus went by La Roche Guyon and Mantes.

The division reserve consisted of the 3rd Battalion of the 315th Infantry, the 304th Engineers Battalion, and the 749th Tank Battalion. We were alerted that we would serve as infantry to

---

[72] Weigley 241

stop the desperate attack to wipe out the Seine bridgehead. This bridgehead, if not destroyed, meant there were few defensible positions between the Seine and the German border. [73]

The bridgehead was enlarged when the British 43rd Division crossed the Seine near Vernon. The 30th Division came into line, relieving some of the 79th positions. General Corlett's XIX Corps took over command of 30th and 79th Divisions on August 29th. The 2nd Armored was added to the XIX Corps. The 304th Engineers Battalion was attached to the 314th Infantry Team, which included the 311th Artillery Battalion.

The order was given to advance to the Belgium border—a distance of 180 miles in three days. One regiment was not completely motorized. We would see troops walking by the side of the road. Trucks would pick up fifty or so and take them twenty miles down the road, then return to pick up fifty more. This was an around-the-clock operation; we spent three days and nights in the truck.

We traveled through many of the battlefields of World War I before we reached the Somme River. The Germans had the Frenchmen dig a series of trenches for several miles. The retreat of the German force was so disorganized and the disaster so complete that they did not even have the time or opportunity to occupy the trenches.

Hitler expected General Model to prepare a new line along the rivers Somme and Marne. Model had General der Flieger Karl Kitzinger, Military Governor of France, at work using organization Todt forces and civilian forces to build the "Kitzinger Line." (Todt forces were labor battalions in the Third Reich named after Fritz Todt, the head of all labor forces. These same labor forces had built the German Autobahn in the

---

[73] History of the 313th 96

1930's.) Model, who did not mince words, had already advised OKW that to hold at the Somme and Marne Rivers he would need thirty divisions plus twelve Panzer divisions. Hitler, though forming new divisions, had no divisions to help Model in the short run, so these trenches were not defended[74]. The entire scene reminded me of the World War I trenches of the history books and movies.

The Germans had blown up the bridge over the Somme River. Company A of the 304th erected a bridge from building lumber and logs found on the site. The Germans had begun an operation to build anti-tank barriers from logs three feet in diameter and twenty feet in length, to be buried to a depth of fifteen feet. We used these logs to make a Jury-rig bridge to get the 313th across. The bridge was completed that night in a driving rain. The regiment had crossed over the Somme during hazardous, blackout conditions by nine the next morning.[75]

General Corlett had ordered all divisions in the XIX Corps to cross the Belgium border by midnight September 2nd after marching night and day. [76]

The drive continued through many small towns and some large citieson the way to Cambrai. As the convoy went through

---

[74] Weigley 255-256
[75] History of the 313th 102
[76] Weigley 275

these towns, we were welcomed by thousands of French people-in some towns the crowd went wild, showering the trucks with flowers, fruit and schnapps.[77]

When we entered Cambrai, the people were completely out of control, which delayed the convoy for two hours. Women who had cohabited with German officers had their heads shaved and were paraded on the streets accompanied by abuse both verbal and physical. Some of them were sent down the street topless.

Two women approached our truck and were asked if they spoke Polish by our chief cocksmen (any city that has coal mines has Polish people in abundance). They answered yes and the next thing we knew, he had jumped out of the truck and entered a nearby house. He emerged from the house after twenty minutes with a big smile on his face, as evidence that the sex was very good. He was fortunate that the truck was in place for him to return to! This incident was the exception as the 79th Division kept tight control over their convoys and did not permit soldiers to leave their trucks.

Although the men in the front line would gripe about their misery, sex was not a major concern in battle. The men at the front were too scared, busy, hungry, tired and demoralized to think about sex at all.[78] In fact, the front was the one wartime place that was sexless. [79]

The rest of the march into Belgium was routine. We arrived in a field near Tournai at 2 a.m. September 3rd, missing the target by two hours.

---

[77] History of the 313th 103
[78] Carafano 55
[79] Fussell 108

Major General Wyche received a commendation for this historic advance from the commanding general of the XIX Corps, Major General Charles H. Corlett.

"On August 28th, 1944, the 79th Infantry Division joined this corps. At that time it had already established a bridgehead and was astride the Seine River. The corps was ordered to advance and in seventy-two hours the division covered a total of 180 miles, crossing the Somme River and numerous smaller streams and closing in perfect order in its objectives in Belgium.

"This is believed to be one of the fastest opposed advances of comparable distance by an infantry division in warfare. It is desired to commend you, your officers and men on this splendid achievement. The Commanding General, U.S. First Army, Lt. General Courtney Hodges concurs in the commendation."

The First Army had run out of gas. In Company A, we had one jeep with gasoline in the tank. We lay around for five days enjoying our new state of leisure. Lt. Colonel Van Allen ordered every solider to get a haircut. Chico, the company barber, had long lines waiting to be sheared. Shower tents were set up to give us a shower, the second one since May 30. Taking two showers in ninety days was pretty good for an army in combat. Morale was sky-high as we all thought the war would soon be over.

SUPPLY AND FUEL CRISIS

The allied victory in France was a quartermaster's worst nightmare. A German general once remarked that the blitzkrieg was paradise for the tactician and hell for the quartermaster. But it was Ernie Pyle who described what follows as a tactician's hell and a quartermaster's purgatory.[80]

---

[80] D'Este 647

The American army divisions were almost totally mobilized, requiring shipping miracles to supply them in a timely manner. The army counted on high firepower and high mobility to make up for the reduced number of divisions—from 106 divisions to a final count of eighty-nine combat divisions created and deployed.

An American division included between 2,322 and 3,698 vehicles. The minimum satisfactory supply of gasoline and lubricants for a division was 6700 tons; and the minimum satisfactory supply of 105mm artillery shells (a ten day supply) weighed 5,582 tons. Just the gasoline and 105mm shells required three or four ships, assuming they all survived the crossing.

Twenty-eight divisions advanced across France and into Belgium. Each division used 750 tons of supplies per day—this worked out to 20,000 tons a day.

Most of a modern army's manpower is dedicated to protecting the force that actually engages in combat...in World War II the United States had 3 million men in Europe of which only 750,000 were combat infantrymen.[81]

The French railroad had been almost totally destroyed in northern France. The army set up the "Red Ball Express" involving 300 truck battalions. Thousands of trucks picked up supplies in Normandy and brought them to the front, a brutal 700-mile, twenty-four hour round trip journey. But the Red Ball Express could deliver only 7,000 tons a day. The Army Air Corps, even with a maximum effort, could deliver only 1,000 tons per day to the front.

However, the greatest supply problem proved to be gasoline. Each of the three armies consumed almost 400,000 gallons of

---

[81] Carafano 47

gasoline a day—proving to be a large number of five gallon cans! An additional problem was the consumption of nearly 300,000 gallons of gas to keep the trucks rolling. Each army captured German gasoline supplies that helped to keep the trucks rolling.

After the breakthrough, German food was issued to supplement the K rations and 5-in-1s. We received large sardines in tomato sauce (which was the best!) and bread and large cans of jam and cheese, which were devoured with relish.

A nurse in the 77th evacuation hospital recalls the enjoyment in eating captured food outside Chartres. She wrote, "Delicious sardines and cheese...the cheese was put in a collapsible tube like toothpaste, and was of a variety which smells so bad, but tastes so good. There were eggs and oranges."[82]

In "Patton's Third Army," Charles Province reported,

> *[August] "The Third Army made arrangements to furnish diesel fuel to French civilians for their tractors, for the harvesting of crops in Brittany."*

> *[September] "The Third Army captured many tons of grain, flour, sugar and rice and also hundreds of carloads of coal were distributed to the French population."*

The Third Army captured a total of 2.6 million pounds of frozen beef and 500 thousand pounds of canned beef, which were issued to the troops at the front." [83]

---

[82] Ambrose, Citizen Soldiers 329
[83] Province 36, 42, 54, 58

COULD THE GERMAN ARMY RECOVER?

General Montgomery's decision to halt at Antwerp had serious consequences. The German Fifteenth Army escaped on September 6 by ferrying 80,000 troops across to Walcheren Island on the north side of the Scheldt Estuary. This was the second time that the allies had permitted a major German force to escape encirclement and destruction. From there, the 15th Army deployed back into Holland to the north of the British army. This provided the Germans with control of the Scheldt Estuary, which the British army was not able to break until late November, 1944. This meant that the allies did not have Antwerp available until very late.[84]

Almost every soldier, from General Eisenhower to the lowest private, thought the war would soon be over, due to the slaughter of the German army in France. They did not know how resilient the Reich would prove to be. Already the Nazi party was introducing a national draft, all universities and colleges in Germany were being closed to raise men for the new "Peoples Grenadier Division" that was assembled to be ready for combat by January 1st, 1945. (See chapter on Nordwind).

German strategic military reserves were to be six divisions. Intelligence indicated that enemy reinforcements were en route from other fronts. Third Army estimated that:

> *"The enemy could bring the equivalent of three divisions with fifty tanks from Italy and four divisions from Denmark and Norway. Four other divisions were reported moving from the Scandinavian countries although no known reinforcements were coming from the Russian front. It is believed that the Germans had the capability of withdrawing an estimated three divisions and 150 tanks from the Eastern front by October 1st, if necessary."* [85]

---

[84] Murray & Millett 438
[85] Province 44

The Luftwaffe's flying schools were closed, as were the U-Boat schools, to release men for the infantry. September 1944 would see the miracle of Albert Speers' war. Production of tanks, planes and guns would reach the highest level of the war. This meant that the new divisions received new equipment. Their supply lines were drastically reduced as the army was now defending the fatherland. The German generals were not going to surrender as long as there was still a chance for victory.[86]

The greatest mistake the allies made in 1944 was to underestimate their opponents' strength. The collapse of the German army had been so sudden and so complete that the allied generals found the idea of a revival of the Wehrmacht forces almost inconceivable. The Soviet generals could have warned their western counterparts that the Germans were all too effective in resurrecting their military forces.

The German fight at Market Garden should have raised warning flags. Optimism was prevalent in the allied command. The leaders looked for that one final push to drive the Germans into the final defeat as the rout of August. It was to prove a long wait.[87]

---

[86] Whiting 66
[87] Murray & Millett 438

11

Third Army XV Corps/ Seventh Army

I will leave the account of the trip south with an account of Operation Dragoon and the makeup of the Sixth Army Group and the Seventh Army.

OPERATION DRAGOON

On August 15th, the American army launched Operation Dragoon with the landing of the French 1st Army and the American Sixth Army group. This operation that pulled three divisions out of Italy was opposed by Churchill and the British chiefs of staff. Churchill favored an attack into "the soft underbelly of Europe," the Balkans. The American chiefs believed that Italy was a sideshow and that strategic and operational results would justify the landing in southern France. The invaders would then drive north to hook with the Third Army in its drive across France. This insistence by American chiefs caused much bad blood with their counterparts, the British chiefs.[88]

The landings were almost without opposition, at a cost of three thousand casualties in the month-long campaign. The Seventh Army came through southern France and hooked up with Patton's Third Army in Lorraine by

---

[88] Murray & Millett 433

September. Critics of the Seventh thought the campaign had been much too easy; they called it the "Champagne Campaign."

While the Seventh had gone through France almost unnoticed by the public back home, Omar Bradley's two armies in the north were in the headlines as they steamed toward the German border. The commander of the Seventh, General Alexander Patch, was a brave and competent officer, but he was no Patton. The Seventh Army continued to be America's forgotten army.[89]

The Americans were right. Dragoon liberated southern France and provided a line that ran from the English Channel to the Swiss border. Most important was the capture of the port city of Marseilles, which solved many supply problems since the French railroads were intact with enough capacity to supply the U.S. forces fighting on the western front through the fall and winter 1944-45. The port of Antwerp was not available to the allies until December.[90] If the port of Antwerp were available earlier, the Battle of the Bulge may not have happened.

THIRD ARMY XV CORPS

On Sept 19th, we joined a huge convoy of 300 vehicles as part of 313th Infantry Regiment with the destination of Reims, France. The convoy went through many towns and villages that were free from war's damages. The trip was largely during night hours, but when the convoy came to Reims we had a good look at one of France's largest cities, paying attention to the beauty and grandeur of the world-famed Reims cathedral, clearly visible in the distance.[91]

---

[89] Whiting 4
[90] Murray & Millett 433
[91] History of the 313th 105

The division was advised we would rejoin Patton's 3rd Army as part of the XV Corps, which included the French 2nd Armored.

After a three-hour rest and refueling, the convoy started up again until we were 10 miles from Neufchateau, when infantry dismounted and marched to an area on the Moselle River.

BACK IN ACTION

The high morale of Belgium was now back to reality, but the men optimistically believed the war would be over before Christmas.

With the French 2nd Armored guarding the army and corps right flank, General Haislip started his drive of September 11th by motorizing the 314th Infantry Regiment and stripping two corps artillery battalions to accomplish the move. He ordered the 313th down the valley from just north of Neufchateau to Charmes. The 79th performed an unusual feat by marching across the front of the German 16th Division. The 314th Regiment captured the town of Charmes in a day-long fight on September 12th.[92] Though the Germans blew the bridges across the Moselle River, B Company of the 304th found a ford over the river.[93]

About this time, our squad was given an assignment in a nearby town. Ten of us jumped in the truck and went roaring down the road. We came upon a sentry blocking the road and telling us to stop. Our wild driver, Hugh Cummings, ignored the order to stop and proceeded down the road for about a half-mile and entered a town. We saw German troops running to greet us. Cummings ordered us to dismount while he turned the truck around. Fortunately the truck had a 30-caliber heavy

[92] Weigley 337
[93] History of the 79th 61

machine gun mounted in front. The gunner fired the machine gun continuously to keep the German soldiers' heads down. The truck got turned around and came back around for us. I will never know how we managed to jump back onto a moving truck. The men already on pulled us into the truck. Poor Chico tried to jump on the side and went through the dual wheels. We couldn't stop to pick him up, but we hoped for the best. We praised God that we were back behind the American lines. Chico also crawled back to the American lines, was sent to a military hospital and never returned. Ever since this episode, when watching movies or films on prisoners of war in Germany, I thank God for the truck-mounted machine gun and our miraculous escape that day.

Hugh Cummings, an Iowa native, was one of the best truck drivers in the army. How he joined is an interesting story. Hugh's cousin told him he had some car tires that Hugh could have. Hugh came to the cousin's place and picked up the tires even though the cousin was not present. The next thing he knew, Hugh was arrested for stealing car tires. When he appeared before the judge for sentencing, the judge told him that if he joined the army, they would drop the charges. He joined the 79th Division shortly after. This option meant thousands of men might have joined the army as an alternative to going to jail.

The 315th Regiment in its drive toward Chatenois met the French 2nd Armored Division, which meant one regiment-sized combat team of the German army was cut off. After intense negotiations, the German colonel agreed to surrender at 10:00 a.m. to General Greer. By 9:50 the complete motorized German regiment was assembled, consisting of eighty-four vehicles (most of them American 2½-ton trucks) in a two mile long column; two 88mm guns, a six-gun battery, forty-five trucks, twenty-nine German jeeps, five motorcycles, two half tracks and three Red Cross trucks.

It was a challenge to get the convoy to the division prisoner of war area without being shot up by U.S. airplanes. Each truck had cerise panels on top. An MP vehicle led the column with another vehicle in back, while German MPs rode up and down the route. Luckily, this convoy arrived at the prisoner enclosure without incident. During the fighting of the next five days, the 79th Division played a key part in destroying the German 16th Division.[94]

LORRAINE GERMAN PRISONERS

Keith E. Bonn reports the situation of German prisoners in the Seventh Army front as follows:

"Faced with the choice of fighting to the last man or to a foe known for his humane treatment of prisoners, it is not surprising that so many German troops opted for the latter. Some Russian and Polish prisoners taken by the advancing echelons of the 103rd Infantry Division said they murdered their German officers so they could surrender. Ersatz coffee, like ersatz discipline, was no replacement but only an unsatisfactory temporary substitute. "The deleterious effect of such ersatz morale on combat proficiency was clearly significant in the increasingly uncomfortable and deadly environment of warfare in the high Vosges."[95]

By the end of September, the 79th Division had captured 15,526 prisoners of war in 102 days of combat.

After three days of hard fighting, the 79th Division captured Luneville—a railroad and highway hub close to the confluence

---

[94] History of the 79th 61-61
[95] Bonn 117

of the Meuhre and Vezouse Rivers—and advanced to the Forest of Parroy. Hitler had fought in the Forest in World War I, so he gave orders that it should be held at all costs.[96]

The Forest of Parroy was a six-mile by five-mile forest defended by the 11th and 15th Panzer Grenadier Divisions. The Germans had build up a continuous line of concrete pill boxes, trenches, and anti-tank ditches.[97]

The attack set for September 25th was to be preceded by a bombing mission. Several days of rain and fog delayed the mission until September 28th. The XIX Tactical Air Command mission lasted for ninety minutes. German prisoners interviewed stated that the results were not effective. On September 29th, the 79th Division was made part of the US 6th Army Group, Seventh Army XV Corps.

---

[96] Bonn 74-75
[97] Whiting 70-71

12

The Seventh Army

The Allied forces facing the German defenders were part of the Sixth Army Group commanded by Lieutenant General Jacob L. Devers, a classmate of George Patton's at West Point in 1909. Lt. Gen. Devers was an artilleryman by experience. Along with many of his fellow officers, he missed combat experience in World War I. His assignments included several tours as an instructor at West Point and the Artillery School at Fort Sill, OK. His major wartime assignment had been serving as Commanding General of the American Army of ETO (European Theater of Operations) from May 1943 until General Eisenhower took over in 1944. General Marshall appointed him to this position despite the coolness of General Eisenhower, who did not wish to deal with him again.[98]

Lt. Gen. Alexander Patch, a class of 1913 graduate of West Point, commanded the Americans on Guadalcanal from May 1942 to January 1943. During that time his division distinguished itself in both offensive and defensive operations in the dripping jungles. General Patch gained further experience when he assumed command of XIV Corps in the Solomon Islands. The lessons of combat in the Pacific islands served him well in the Vosges difficult terrain against an experienced enemy.[99]

---

98 Bonn 68, 69
99 Bonn 70

The XV Corps was commanded by Major General Wade H. Haislip of the class of 1912, a career infantryman who saw action on the western front in World War I. His prior WWII experience was as a member of the War Department General Staff and as Commanding General of the 85th Division.

The 79th Division had been assigned to the XV Corps during the breakthrough in Normandy. This produced a large degree of cohesion between Haislip and Wyche.[100]

The acquisition of the XV Corps, despite General Devers' optimism and enthusiasm, still had many problems. Both the VI and the XV Corps were exhausted and also had serious logistical problems. After more than 100 days of combat, the units of the 79th Division were very tired and the division was short many items of supply and equipment. Each of the three regiments was below their authorized strength of 3,348 men; the 313th was short by 575 men, the 314th by 360 men and the 315th by 600 men. The artillery battalions were short of ammunition and well-trained men. After visiting the 79th, General Devers estimated that Wyche would need at least two weeks out of the line for rest and to receive replacements. But for the moment, however, the division could not be withdrawn from the front.[101]

The manpower problems of the U.S. Army grew out of the decision to settle for only eighty-nine divisions instead of 106; this decision meant that there was an acute shortage of manpower to cover the front from Holland to Switzerland. This meant that the American army had problems pulling divisions from the front lines for rest and refitting because every division was needed to hold the line. The 7th Army, however, pulled their weary divisions off the line for from between seven and

---

[100] Bonn 74, 75
[101] Clarke & Smith 254

fourteen days of rest and training. There was virtually no reserve. Thus American divisions remained in battle for the duration of the fighting in Europe. While individuals joined them in combat after a brief stay in replacement depots (called "Repple Depples" in the lingo of the victims) in their new units, these fresh replacements found themselves friendless and alone during their initial combat experience. The American manpower shortage was exacerbated by the army's retention of too many support troops, who could easily have served in combat without a serious impact on the logistical structure.[102]

As an example of the magnitude of the problem, replacements in the Third Army for 281 days of combat were 258,924.[103]

Stephen Ambrose in Citizen Soldiers said "the GIs bitterly resented the replacement and reinforcement policies that assigned men as individuals to combat units. The replacements paid the cost of receiving no training, which resulted in 50% becoming casualties in their first three days." In the good outfits, old timers took charge and accepted and trained them to fit into an existing squad. [104]

In our squad, it fell to Sergeant Willie Nale, Tech/Sergeant James Johnson and me to see to it that replacements were trained to be a part of the squad. In Alsace, during Nordwind, one man was with us for a week before he discovered I was a PFC and not a sergeant.

---

[102] Murray & Millett 457
[103] Province 294
[104] Ambrose 287, 288

THE FOREST OF PARROY

After the bombing, as the 313th and the 315th entered the forest, all hell broke loose when Mark IV tanks raced down a road attacking the surprised American infantrymen. The German counterattack had begun!

As night fell, all was confusion and panic in the wet and foggy forest. Snipers and infiltrators were everywhere. Shock groups of Grenadiers, armed with machine pistols and grenades, attacked the American infantry with savage action where neither side gave an inch of ground. The Germans then disappeared in the trees.[105]

By October 1st, the 313th and 315th were one-third of the way through the forest, facing strong counter-attacks almost every step of the way. We in Company A built two roads, usually reserved for corps engineers under artillery fire, a road that took us five days to construct. We hauled 1000 two-and-a-half ton loads. My group worked for thirty-six hours straight digging gravel to load the truck and resting until the truck returned. This routine continued night and day regardless of our state of exhaustion. Gallows-type humor helped us keep on working even when we thought we could not move a muscle.

The Germans had vision on the existing road, so we laid a corduroy road for about a quarter mile by cutting down trees of eight inches in diameter, then placing them side-by-side across. A log was put in place every ten feet or so to secure the road. We worked in constant rain and became wet to the skin. I wasn't good at the ax, so I carried the logs and put them into place. For three long days, our team chopped some 3000 eight-inch logs by hand to cover the 500 yards. In the end, that finished road got U.S. vehicles across muddy ground.

---

[105] Charles Whiting 70-71

The day the road was completed, one American ambulance came over the road with the tires bumping over each log. The front moved enough to make our log road no longer necessary.[106]

The constant rain produced muddy roads reminding me of Minnesota mud in the spring. The American 2½-ton truck was equipped with a winch strong enough to pull the truck through the mud. We would attach the cable to a tree and winch the truck from tree to tree until the truck was back on the road.

On October 9th, the final attack on the forest (again in a driving rain) began, supported by artillery tanks and tank destroyers. The Germans were firing from dugouts and other fortifications. It took an attack from all sides to subdue the defenders.[107]

General George C. Marshall visited the 79th Division to witness the attack.

SEVENTH ARMY SUPPLY PROBLEMS

Just as logistical limitations forced the 3rd Army to stall, so too were the long lines leading to the Vosges Mountains from the ports of Marseilles and Toulon stretched to the breaking point. With six divisions to support and growing distances to cover, the 7th Army supply situation at the time of Patch's September 29th directives would not permit an immediate major attack.

By the first week in October, the American supply situation reached a critical situation. Strict controls were placed on supply rates to all units of the 7th Army: fifteen to twenty rounds per artillery gun per day. Clearly no offensive could be started with such constraints.

[106] History of the 79th 43
[107] History of the 79th 72

By the end of the second week in October, these problems had been largely corrected. A combination of a reorganized supply system, and the establishment of supply distribution facilities closer to the front at Charms, Mirecourt and Epinelle, caused the logistical situation to improve. Now General Truscott was willing to launch the attack, but this delay had given the German Nineteenth Army time to prepare their defenses in depth along the Vosges Mountains.[108]

After clearing the forest, we came to a more open, hilly ground. The objective was to capture Embermenil and Fort de Mannonviller. The battle raged for four days, with the Germans attacking with heavy artillery concentration. Sherman tanks would attack with infantry support, only to bog down in the fields of mud.[109]

Two companies of the 315th received presidential citations for bravery during the fighting at Embermenil. The Lorraine Cross, the newspaper of the 79th Division published on June 26th and August 1, 1945, described the action:

> *"First presidential Citation: Company A, 315th Infantry Regiment is cited for the extraordinary gallantry and heroism in moving against overwhelmingly superior enemy numbers and fire to seize and hold the high ground east of Embermenil, France during the period 20 October 1944 to 22 October 1944."*

The men remembered two seemingly endless, action-filled days and nights that found the German soldiers defying cold steel and hand-to hand-fighting. When it was all over, clean-up squads discovered dead GIs and Germans in the same foxholes.

---

[108] Bonn 87

[109] History of the 79th 74

Staff Sgt. Anonte C. Soars, wounded in Embermenil, remembered, "After we had started up the hill, my whole squad was pinned down by a Jerry machine gun. Then I saw something that revived my faith in God and the M-1. Although pinned down, my boys brought fire to bear with their rifles and first thing you know, those same Krauts were pinned down. I took a couple of men and circled around to capture the six man crew."

The battle of Embermenil ended after twenty-four hours with German casualties of thirty dead and 175 wounded. 315th Infantry casualties were ten killed and forty-seven wounded.

By its own heroic action in storming, seizing, and holding a strategic high point against overwhelming enemy superiority, Company A contributed in a large way to the success of the 315th Regiment.[110] Company F of the 315th Infantry also received a presidential citation for the same battle.[111] German casualties—nineteen prisoners, nineteen wounded, and 200 killed.

MANURE

During October 1944, General Patton was despondent. The XV Corps had been taken away and given to the 7th Army to the south. He disliked Lorraine—a nasty country where it rained every day and the whole wealth of the people existed in assorted manure piles.

In Lorraine and Alsace, the farmers or peasants lived in small villages. The lower floors of many houses served as a barn for the cows. The heat from the cows kept the second floor—where many families lived—from being so cold. In warm weather, the cows were driven to fields outside the town; in cold weather, the cows stayed in the barn.

---

[110] Cross of Lorraine: Vol 1 No 3
[111] Cross of Lorraine: Vol 1 No 2

Manure piles were on the cobblestone streets near every house. When it rained, as it did every day, it seemed during 1944, the street flowed with a manure-like liquid, which smelled very bad when it got on our boots. The farmers often wore wooden shoes outside of their homes and slippers inside.

KITCHEN

Our kitchen had not been with us since England. Once the front was stabilized, we got the kitchen and the crew back.

The first night they set up in an old barn, using flashlights for lighting. One cook poured soup in our pint-sized cup, which we were expected to drink before we reached the end of the chow line. Then they poured coffee flavored with condensed milk and sugar into the same cup. If you weren't careful, you could easily fall prey to the cooks' favorite prank: pouring coffee into the unfinished cup of soup, knowing what a disgusting mess this would cause. In the morning, they would fill up our cups with unsweetened grapefruit juice. (Grapefruit juice with cognac was an excellent cold-weather fighting drink).

A few days later, the kitchen moved to a limestone building off a courtyard. We lined up early; the smell of sausage and eggs was almost too much. This was the first time we had eaten a cooked, hot breakfast since our company left England in May 1944.

As we waited in line, our breakfast reverie was quickly interrupted by shells, which came in hitting near the courtyard. Shrapnel bounced off the cobblestones. Most everyone ran at the sound of shells. I ignored the attack and went into the building to enjoy my breakfast. Soon I was joined by the rest of the company as they got their courage back.

One night we slept in a mow, filled with hay. As we placed our blankets on the hay and got ready to enjoy a good night's sleep, I heard an odd sound. I got out a flashlight and quickly trained my beam on the source of the noise—a large rat making its way down the wall. I covered my head with my blanket and waited for the rat to come by. He ran over my blanket, and to this day I still hate rats.

THE BRIDGE FIASCO

The Germans blew a wooden trestle bridge of about twenty-five feet in length and sixteen feet high, and we were assigned to rebuild it. Each engineering company had a lumber trailer, with enough lumber to construct a bridge to hold thirty tons-roughly the weight of a Sherman tank.

Cutting the big ten-inch by fourteen-inch timbers for the double trestle consumed much of the morning. Finally the sixteen foot-high trestle was finished and ready to set up. After a huge struggle, we managed to put the trestle in place, only to find that the carpenter had used inside measurements instead of outside measurements, making our bridge twelve inches too short. (I had never heard such cursing and vulgar remarks as that very moment!) One day later, a new lumber supply was found and the bridge was finished without incident.

MINE FIELDS

Several days later, Company A, Third Platoon was requested to mark a minefield in a large, open field. The Germans laid regal mines (a long box type-about two feet long and weighing ten to fifteen pounds). We marked each mine with white flags and posted mine signs.

After marking the mines, we saw the outlines of human forms. Moving forward, we stumbled on two dead German soldiers who had been run over by a tank. Their bodies had been squashed, and were about two feet wide. The memory of this gruesome sight has never quite left me, even after almost sixty years. On Veterans' Day, 2001, I sat in a church listening to a pastor recount how the Germans, even to this day, grieved over their war dead. The next moment a vivid flashback took me back to 1944, that minefield, and the gruesome discovery of those bodies.

REST AT LAST

On October 25th, after 127 days of combat, the 44th Division relieved the 79th Division. The Lorraine Campaign caused the division 2,016 casualties.

The 304th Engineers Battalion went into a camp near Luneville. We were all bone-tired and spent the first few days relaxing. We also got to enjoy our third shower and fourth change of underwear since June. We cleaned our equipment, including company tools, etc. We received passes to visit Luneville, a large cathedral city. The lights were on and the stores were open. I still have several post cards of Luneville.

The history of the 313th Infantry reported, "Everywhere you went the beer halls were full, and in the areas where the troops where bivouacked, you could find groups of men staging shindigs of their own using company funds for the purchase of beer and other spirits." [112] I did not participate in any of these activities, and have no way of knowing whether some of my platoon mates did or not.

---

[112] History of the 313th 130, 131

Soldiers appreciated any break in action and even a short withdrawal from fighting permitted hot rations, mail call, sleep, and a bath or a shower. A simple shower became a real treat for troops that had not changed clothes for weeks, or even months, at a time.

A few days away from combat also meant sorely needed sleep. One soldier slept for thirty-six hours after weeks in line under miserable conditions.[113] Ernie Pyle was amazed at how fast the men bounced back. "The startling thing to me about these rest periods was how quickly the human body could recuperate from critical exhaustion, how rapidly the human mind snapped back to the normal state of laughing, grousing, yarn-spinning, and yearning for home."[114]

While the order for training was not appreciated, since an order is an order, we went through the motions—the time was spent integrating replacements into the life of each squad and platoon. Winter clothing was issued; we had to make do with the old cloth overcoats and caps until we received new jackets and boots in December. Clean blankets were also issued. PFC Oldham had to turn in some of the ten blankets he had accumulated! Many were stained with mud and manure from sleeping in foxholes and cow pastures. We placed our bedrolls in the truck every time we moved on. It was beginning to seem as though we really could get used to almost anything.

Keith Bonn, in *"When the Odds were Even"* discusses the winter conditions in Alsace in November and December 1944 and into 1945:

"It has been said that the two armies in winter must face the same conditions and that the weather favors no one. But

---

[113] Kindsvatter, 94, 95
[114] Pyle 286

from mid-October 1944 to Mid-January 1945 the weather clearly favored the dogged defenders of the Vosges. Although the temperatures in the Vosges were not that extreme (ranging from thirty-eight to sixty-eight degrees in October, 25 to 60 degrees in November, 15 to forty-three degrees in December, and consistently below freezing in January. Daily rain and considerable winds during the period created conditions that made living in the open an extremely hazardous and miserable experience for the frequently exposed American infantrymen." [115]

We were issued new combat coats, water-resistant and well-insulated with fabric, new winter caps with earflaps, new water-resistant fatigues, and new combat boots with rubber soles. The new jackets had a tie around the middle to keep heat in, the sleeves also had wool inserts to keep out the cold (the old wool overcoat let cold air in through the sleeves and collar). The hood attached to the jacket could be worn over or under the helmet (see picture from 79th Division History).

New insulated bedrolls were issued to replace blankets. Affectionately called fart sacks, a good number of GIs were killed or captured by the Germans in their sleeping bags when surprised as they slept. Combat soldiers often slept on top of the bedroll with blankets over them. New raincoats were issued that also doubled as shelter halves.

When watching films of the Battle of the Bulge, I noticed most of the GIs wore the old overcoats, shoes and wool caps. General Bradley chose ammunition over winter clothing in October 1944, assuming the war would be over before winter clothing would be needed. The First Army men paid a larger price for this decision in frostbite and trench foot. [116]

---

[115] Bonn 26
[116] Murray & Millett 462

Top left: A New Lieutenant
Champagne and PFC Namath
Franzenbad, Czechoslovakia

Top right: Staff Sgt. McIntosh
Camp Laguna

Bottom left: A Rare Moment of
Rest Senior Lieutenant William
Klimek

13

Vosges to Alsace

After the Forest of Parroy, the land became hilly, open land with trees growing in small forests. Major General Haislip, Commander of the XV Corps, issued an order on November 8 directing his corps on the German Army in the Saverne Gap (a pass through the Vosges Mountains). The XV Corps would attempt to get through the Saverne Gap defenses and surround the forces defending the Gap.

The 79th was assigned the main attack to the northeast from Hablainville to capture Sarrebourg, which would penetrate the first of the four defensive belts in the Saverne Gap. This was defended by the 21st Panzer Division. To avoid the main force of the German 19th Army, the 79th Division would drive across the Vesouze River to Blamond and trap the 5530 Volksgrenadier Division.

The 314th encountered great difficulty near Barbas because the bridge had been blown by the Germans as they retreated. Company A of the 304th Engineers Battalion built a treadway bridge. I remember that we had to cease work several times when artillery rounds came in too close for comfort. The next day the bridge was completed when our artillery laid down a barrage heavy enough to silence the German fire.[117]

---

[117] History of the 79th 83

During the battle for the Saverne Gap, German communications trucks containing the 19th Army communications equipment were captured, which would prove disastrous in the Nordwind campaign, discussed later in this book.

General Haislip assigned General LeClerc's Second Armored Division the task of breaking through the Gap made by the 79th Division. (The 79th Division and the Second Armored Division were a team in the breakout, and after) The French Second Armored Division would drive through Sarrebourg and into the Saverne Gap. Divisions of the XV Corps would surround the German units remaining in the Vosges and then drive toward Strasbourg.[118]

I don't remember much of the drive through the Saverne Gap and into the Alsatian plain; but I do remember the trip over the Saverne Gap as we were on our way to Pont-a-Mousson for a two-week rest. The next two weeks were spent fighting our way through the forest of Hagenau and towns of Bischweiler-Hagenau.

The German air activity hit a new peak with fifty-two sorties made over the division area. The 463rd Anti-Aircraft Artillery Battalion shot down seven planes. As the planes flew over, we shot at them with rifles and machine guns.[119]

One memorable story of dubious veracity of the battle for Hagenau made the rounds in my company. The 79th Division had captured Hagenau after a bitter battle in the Hagenau Forest. One of the first areas taken was the railroad station. The telephone rang and a German-speaking American sergeant answered the phone. Permission was requested to bring a German troop train into the station and was quickly granted.

---

[118] Bonn 112, 114
[119] History of the 79th 88

As soon as the train pulled into the station, it was captured by infantry and 300 troops were taken prisoner, proving that in wartime, things moved so fast that the German army did not always know when a particular resource or area had fallen to the American army.

The Champagne Campaign was over; now the autumn rains were falling nearly every day. The war was now a slow, slogging match with weary men going through hills and mud against a well-dug-in German army.

As Charles E. Whiting described the new situation by quoting a GI:

> *"The beautiful babes weren't beautiful any more. The happy healthy people were hungry and thin. ...as for scenery, that forest full of Christmas trees were lousy with snipers; those winding streams running through the valleys...only made their feet wetter and the full moon shone on the hills...making the GIs curse, thinking of the long climb and the mud and more mud on the other sidel."[120] The time of despair had clearly started."*

The troops noticed the change in the people in the villages and small towns in the plains below, which they were now liberating. They found many cities where speech, dress and customs were predominantly German. Now the VI Corps had to watch for spies, snipers, and German sympathizers, many of whom were women.

GERMAN PRISONERS

As the fighting approached the borders of the fatherland in the Vosges Mountains, many of the German troops believed

---

[120] Whiting 71

the war was already lost. Every US division captured thousands of prisoners who simply deserted during this part of the campaign—a sure indicator of declining morale. In spite of decreasing morale, German units fought well, at least at first, and no division-sized units collapsed completely (see chapter thirteen on the surrender of a German regiment to the 79th Division).

According to U.S. estimates at that point in the war, the fighting zeal of German units was motivated to a significant extent by fear of punishment, shame, and even fear of reprisal against family members in Germany. In an estimate written in early November 1944, Seventh Army intelligence officers concluded that although most German officers still followed orders out of a sense of duty, pride and professionalism, the ordinary soldier was different. German soldiers fighting for their lives in the Vosges were often blatantly intimidated by their superiors to performing well on the battlefield.

Executions were routinely carried out pursuant to courts-martial that found soldiers absent from their units guilty of "attempted desertion." As part of the Wehrmacht's campaign to discourage desertion, the deadly results of sentencing were widely publicized throughout the German units by the chain of command. Prisoners reported instances of threats, beatings, and even shootings of German units by SS units located directly behind army defensive units.[121] The 79th Division processed more than 35,000 German prisoners through its prisoner of war gate from June 23rd, 1944 to May 8th, 1945.[122]

---

[121] Bonn 115, 116
[122] Lorraine July 14, 1945

MUD, MUD and MORE MUD

One rainy, cold day, our squad was walking down a road in combat formation (fifteen feet between each soldier). Suddenly a shell hit the shoulder of the road not three feet from me. Soldiers say that you never hear a shell that hits you, and I certainly did not hear this one. Fortunately, the shell hit the mud and then the tar road, which absorbed the shell and shrapnel. (I consider this the 5th of my nine lives). The other members of the squad could hardly believe I was not harmed by a shell that was normally close enough to kill me. From that point onward, I was considered a good luck charm, with men advising one another to stand near me to be safe from shells.

Another cold, misty day, our task was to repair a bridge damaged by shells. As we dismounted from the truck, a battery of 240mm howitzers fired with a terrific noise. All but one of us recognized the noise as that of an outgoing barrage, but my friend Oldham thought it was incoming, so he jumped into a hole by the side of the road. The Germans had six-foot holes dug for their troops to jump in, to aid them in hiding from American planes. The foxhole was filled with rainwater, and he sank to the bottom before pulling himself out, freezing and shivering. He stuttered, "Does anyone have a cigarette?" We made him stay until the bridge job was finished in late afternoon. He was sick by that time, and went to the hospital. He came back to us only when the war was over.

At one point, a stomach flu virus went through the company. One night we were sleeping in a big warehouse building with a long walk to the latrine. I had laid down for the night and zipped up the zipper on the sleeping bag, prepared for a good night's sleep. Suddenly, I felt sick and threw up my dinner, and then had to go at the other end as well.

This really fouled up the sleeping bag! I don't remember how I cleaned the bag, or if perhaps I was issued a new one.

BASEMENT

We pulled into a cold basement late at night. I don't remember why we did not have our bedrolls with us. There were many bunk beds in the large room. We each got into a bunk bed and tried to curl up in our warm overcoat. This was less than satisfactory, so I pulled the mattress from the top bunk and put it on top of me. This mattress was heavy, but it kept me warm.

Then someone had the bright idea to start a fire in an empty barrel. However, they failed to consider the problem of what to do about the resultant smoke, which was solved when someone else had the bright idea to break out several windows.

ROADBLOCKS

The 7th Army learned in the high Vosges that pursuing a foe in thick woods and mountainous terrain in fall or winter was certainly a difficult task. Roads through the mountains are few and far between, so highly mobile forces can be slowed by a few well-placed log roadblocks. If the roadblocks are supplemented by mines, machine guns and artillery fire, destruction of these obstacles can drain the resources of an attacker, allowing time for the enemy to regroup, fortify the next position, and gain valuable rest.

From Normandy to Alsace, the 304th Combat Engineers ran across many such roadblocks prepared by the Germans as they retreated. These roadblocks were of two basic types.

France is famous for many of its roads having trees planted alongside them in a regular pattern. They would fell the trees across the road alternating each tree on each side. The largest one of these contained fifty or more logs. Fortunately none of these that we encountered were defended by German troops. To overcome these roadblocks we would saw the trees into smaller logs, which we could winch away with our $2\frac{1}{2}$ ton trucks.

The other type of roadblock was an individual roadblock...a large post that would be drilled directly into the asphalt with a gate as wide as a car, made out of timbers. Each time the Germans had retreated and did not have roadblocks covered by fire, we used the D6 dozer and Diamond T truck to pull out the logs and remove the roadblocks.

LARGE BARRACKS

We were housed in former German army barracks, a large plain building comprised of five or six floors. We received strong warnings to place black out blinds in every window—and told that we had to be careful in our use of lights due to a German railroad 12" gun hidden in a tunnel. It would come out, fire five or six shells and retreat back into the tunnel. We heard the shells go over the building sounding like a flying boxcar. One night a shell hit an upper floor with an awful explosion and the sound of running feet. The next morning we viewed a large hole in the building, and the Company in the space gone.

12" railroad gun captured in Alsace

SNIPERS

On the Seventh Army front in Alsace, the art of sniping reached a new high in the number of victims claimed. In Hagenau, line company doughboys found sniping a pleasant and rewarding means of killing both time and Germans.

The snipers used both the M-1 and the 03 rifles with an evenly-divided opinion of each rifle's performance. The best of the snipers came from K Company 313th Infantry. They were dug in on a quiet front, when a single file of Krauts started across a road fronting the company area. One of the riflemen dropped the leader. The rest of the German line retreated without further incident.

A German appeared waving a Red Cross flag, rushed to the fallen soldier and dragged him away. Some minutes later, this routine replayed itself four or more times. Before it was over, the sniper had hit eighteen soldiers.

The best sniper story occurred in forest of Parroy in October. A Fox Company sergeant spotted a German soldier with two

American prisoners in tow heading for the German lines. The range was 250 yards. The German soldier kept the Sergeant between himself and the American line. When he saw an opening, he squeezed one off. The German guard staggered and fell, and the prisoners raced for American lines and safety in nothing flat.[123]

The last part of November and early December were spent going through towns with Heim and Weiler suffixes.

DUBIOUS DECISION

On November 19th, the French reached the Rhine River and by November 24th orders went out alerting river-crossing units to move forward to assembly areas by the afternoon of the 24th, ostensibly in preparation for the Sixth Army group crossing the Rhine River in force.

Generals Devers and Patch planned a Rhine crossing between the 10th and 20th of December. Generals Eisenhower and Bradley met with Devers and Patch at Luneville. They found VI Corps staff planning the crossing. Eisenhower halted any planning with an immediate order. Devers would argue vigorously that not crossing the Rhine would miss a great opportunity, but both Eisenhower and Bradley stood firm and ordered the 7th Army to turn north to help Patton in his drive to the Roer River. Subsequently Patton confided to staff that Patch's 7th Army should have pushed VI Corps across the Rhine.

Discussing the situation thirty years later, Lt. General Garrison H. Davidson, the 7th Army Engineer who would have been responsible for moving 7th Army across the Rhine on a two-division or eight-battalion front, said that the 7th Army

---

[123] Lorraine Cross Vol 1 No. 3, June 26, 1945

had provided Eisenhower with the opportunity to leave his broad front strategy and make a lightning thrust across the Rhine into the Rastatt area. (The divisions stationed in the Rastatt area, the 45th and the 79th, most likely would have been chosen.)

A strong drive up the east bank of the Rhine might have forced Hitler to divert forces to be used in the Battle of the Bulge to prevent the complete destruction of Army Group B. Once again, General Eisenhower had chosen an operations strategy of firepower and attrition rather than a war of opportunistic maneuver![124]

THANKSGIVING

Thanksgiving Day dawned overcast and cold, with the temperature well below freezing at noon. We lined up outside a stone house, went through a line, and then outside to eat our traditional meal of turkey and mashed potatoes. Since there was no place to sit, we sat on a frozen manure pile. We cracked many jokes on our high cuisine for Thanksgiving and how the atmosphere was conducive for enjoying the meal. Many men talked of past Thanksgivings with a description of the meal and the relatives with whom they shared the meal. It was so cold that I had to stir the canned peaches with my gloved hand to keep them from freezing.

The 79th Division entered Germany at Lauterbourg on December 9th, 1944. I remember entering Germany on a sunny, warm December day. A sign that we placed in the ground read, "You are now entering Germany through the courtesy of the 79th Infantry Division." (The 45th Division

---

[124] Clarke & Smith 439-445

had entered Germany elsewhere two hours before the 79th and made a similar sign).

The 79th made a concerted effort to pierce the Siegfried Line from December 9th to the 15th, 1944 but found the fortifications formidable with machine guns, mortars, and artillery zeroed in on attacking American infantry.

The 313th Infantry encountered a wide anti-tank ditch about twelve feet across. Company A tank dozer, under the command of Lieutenant Smith, filled in the ditch with two paths for infantry to cross while under attack from machine guns and mortar fire. The battle that followed was the worst yet that the 313th had faced. Two to three hundred rounds of artillery came in on two occasions.[125] The attack on the 313th, 314th, and 315th also bogged down the 45th, 79th, 103rd Divisions and 14th Armored, as they each vied in sending barrages into Germany.[126]

---

[125] History of the 313th 147, 148
[126] Whiting 88, 89

14

Battle for Alsace-Nordwind

The front was more or less stable after December 16th with the German attack in Luxembourg. We celebrated Christmas and New Years in a quiet manner. On New Years Eve, the squad of thirteen men formed a circle at midnight. The sergeant passed a quart of cognac and each man took a pull and the bottle barely got around.

On New Years Day I visited a corps battery of 8" guns that were located in an adjacent field and spoke at length with a soldier who told me about the 8" gun. Later in 1948 as a graduate student at the University of Minnesota, I sat next to a man and watched the Gophers practice in Memorial Stadium. After looking at him, we determined that we had met before. After a few minutes, we worked out that we had talked that New Years Day, 1945, in Alsace.

THE VERDUN CONFERENCE

On Tuesday, December 19th, General Eisenhower called the generals together to decide what to do to stop the German breakthrough in Luxembourg. The battle situation was presented with much discussion. The British generals were very concerned with the 1st and 9th Armies split from the Third and Seventh Armies to the south.

Eisenhower turned to General Patton and said "George, I want you to go to Luxembourg and take charge of the battle, making a strong counterattack with at least six divisions. When can you start?"

"As soon as you are through with me" answered Patton, in his usual cocky, brash manner.

According to General Strong, "There was some laughter around the table, especially from the British present." To them, it seemed Patton's reaction was rash and unrealistic. To achieve his aim, Patton would have to swing his Third Army around in a 90-degree angle from its position in Lorraine and the Saar. As it was later discovered, this would mean moving 133,179 vehicles over 1.6 million miles in the worst winter weather in over twenty-five years.

Eisenhower again asked Patton, "When can you start?" and without the slightest hesitation, Patton answered "the morning of the 22nd."[127]

Most of the attention was focused on the star performer, General Patton, and his bold statements, but there was another great general present who went almost completely unnoticed by everyone. It can be argued that General Devers was to play as great a role as Patton in the battle to come. For if the Seventh Army had been defeated at Nordwind, not only would the Third Army's drive into the southern part of the bulge have failed, but the whole western alliance might have collapsed. That Nordwind was stopped was due to the strength of the 6th Army Group and the Seventh Army commanded by General Patch.[128]

---

[127] Whiting 92
[128] Whiting 93

The Verdun Conference concluded by General Eisenhower ordering the 7th Army to break off the attack against the Siegfried Line and to take over the positions in Lorraine vacated by the 3rd Army.

The 7th Army then occupied an eighty-four mile front— from a few miles of Saarbrucken in Germany, then a flanking position north and south of Strasbourg along the Rhine River. The VI Corps held the line from the Rhine to the city of Bitche with the 45th and 79th Divisions and the 14th Armored in reserve. On the left flank on a front of ten miles with little more than a regiment, was task force Huddelson (named after its commander) on the left flank. XV Corps held the line westward to within miles of Saarbrucken with the 100th, 44th and 103rd Divisions. The 106th Cavalry kept a very loose contact with the 3rd Army. The front along the Rhine covered a forty-mile stretch with two regimental task forces who had recently arrived. These totally green soldiers that had never seen combat were known by the names of Task Force Heren (70th Division) and Task Force Linden (42nd Division).

It was an enormous front of eighty-four miles of rugged terrain to hold with six divisions even for veteran soldiers. But for the most part, General Patch's men weren't even veterans. Apart from the 45th and 79th Divisions, they had seen little action. The 44th, 103rd and the 14th Armored had been tested in combat only in the last month. But the new men of the 42nd, 63rd and 70th Divisions were as green as grass.[129] (See appendix on unit cohesion on these divisions in combat.)

On Sunday December 26th, General Devers met with General Eisenhower to report that he was about to be attacked by Germans along his lightly defended front. General Eisenhower

---

[129] Whiting 95

ordered him to put up token resistance and then retreat to Vosges. Under no account was he to permit large American formations to be cut off or surrounded.[130]

That afternoon Eisenhower summoned his fiery Chief of Staff Bedell Smith and told him to tackle Devers. The Sixth Army Group commander was not following his instructions. "You must tell Devers," he informed Bedell Smith angrily, "he is not doing what he was told to do, that is to get VI Corps back and to hold the Alsace Plain with recon and observation elements." ... What Eisenhower, the "political" general par excellence, seemed to forget when he gave this order was the position of Strasbourg. Besides being the capital of Paris, Strasbourg ranked second in French hearts. It was here that Roget de Lisle composed the Marseillaise in 1792. The French had retaken Strasbourg in November, 1944 and were not going to give it up in January without a fight.[131]

General de Gaulle wrote a letter to General Eisenhower declaring that the "French Government cannot...let Strasbourg fall into enemy hands again without first doing everything possible to prevent it. Whatever happens the French will defend Strasbourg."

Next he sent a telegram to both Churchill and Roosevelt drawing their attention to the serious consequences of any withdrawal in Alsace.[132] General de Gaulle threatened that France would not let the US use the French railroads. Smith said that the US would not supply France with ammunition or gasoline. A meeting was set up with de Gaulle, Winston Churchill and General Eisenhower. Churchill agreed with de Gaulle on the importance of Alsace. Eisenhower finally gave in and agreed that there would be no general withdrawal.[133]

---

[130] Whiting 96
[131] Whiting 110
[132] Whiting 111
[133] Whiting 116

On that same day, Hitler ordered the German forces in the Saar to attack the American sweep through the Saverne Gap in the Vosges to link up with the German Nineteenth Army now in the Colmar Pocket, thereby trapping the 7th Army.[134]

On January 1st, 1945 the German offensive named Nordwind started with an attack on the 45th Division on the left flank of the 79th Division in the vicinity of Bitche. The VI Corps ordered the 79th to withdraw to the Maginot Line and to send four battalions to enable the 45th Division to withstand the attack. The first and second battalions of the 313th and the first battalion of the 314th and 315th were sent.

To strengthen the divisions' depleted numbers, regiments from the new 70th were attached. The division started the withdrawal to the fortifications of the Maginot Line on January 7th, 1945. The 304th Engineers Battalion worked night and day laying minefields and putting in defensive obstacles and blowing bridges after our troops had withdrawn.[135]

When the order came to withdraw to positions near the Maginot Line, the 304th Engineer's job was to lay mines in the border area. The first squad laid American Teller mines and anti-personnel mines in a wooded area. We did not have the proper igniters, so we used a box type, which we had to straighten out the pin and the trip wire. We knew this was very dangerous, and sure enough one of the men hit the trip wire. The device exploded, killing Platoon Sergeant Jacobsen and wounding Tech Corporal Johnson. We went through Sergeant Jacobsen's billfold to remove pictures of his girlfriend in England. The army did not send any pictures home, as many wives had been hurt by pictures of other women.

---

[134] Whiting 99
[135] History of the 79th 96

Our other job was to make the pillboxes of the Maginot Line ready for use by the infantry. One large pillbox had a large barn built in front since 1940 which blocked the line of fire, so we were ordered to destroy the barn. We placed 400 lbs of TNT in the barn. Since I was in charge of the detail, I blew the charge with the igniter and the resulting blast was huge. It broke almost every window in town. I can still hear the sound of breaking glass and the women of the town cursing us in both French and German. A green layer of powdered alfalfa hay settled on our clothing and covered the ground for about twenty to thirty minutes.

We were told that all of the houses in one part of town had been destroyed by artillery barrage in 1939. Empty spaces were evidence of all that remained of a town. The Maginot Line was prepared for occupancy by one battalion. Tank destroyers were dug in using our dozer.

Another platoon picked up American Teller mines (teller is the German word for plate) from a depot. The Teller mine weighed twelve pounds and to arm the mine, one unscrewed the protective plate, inserted a fuse the size of a "C" battery, then attached and twisted the cover. Since the mines had been sitting outside in cold, rainy weather, the ice had frozen in the fuse hole. When the caps were tightened, the ice exploded the mine, killing several men. The remains were barely enough to fill a K-ration box.

One of the men injured by a Teller mine explosion was Lt. Hardart. A favorite officer with the men, he was a 1944 graduate of West Point. Although he was the wealthy young heir to the Horne and Hardart cafeterias, he was a common type of man who considered the enlisted men's dignity, and believed they should be treated with respect. He did not pull his rank, but he consulted the men's viewpoint before deciding on a course of action. It was a real blow to the morale of everyone when our favorite officer went down. After the war, I was going to find out his condition in life. I even went into a Horne and Hardart cafeteria, but did not ask any questions.

Later on, we laid hundred of these mines in the deep snow.

Operation Nordwind started January 1, 1945 by hitting the Seventh Army, which involved fifteen U.S. divisions or 250,000 men.[136] The first attack on January 1, 1945 came through the Bitche-Saareguemine, a rough forested area defended by Task Force Hudelson made up of battalions from the 14th Armored and assorted units. This task force defended a line of 10 miles with 2,000 men through an area that was considered the least passable terrain for an enemy attack.

To stop this breakthrough of the German army, General Patch placed General Frederick, commander of the 45th Division, in charge of American forces. This tough ex-paratrooper threw every unit he could find to close the gap in the US lines. He selected the new 12th Armored Division, and several battalions from 313th and 314th regiments of the 79th Division. The new 63rd and 70th Divisions were sent into the line. General Fredericks knew that the vital Saverne Gap had to be held at all costs. For if the Germans had driven

---

[136] Ambrose, Citizen Solders 86

through the gap their Panzers could have turned south to link up with the German troops out of the Colmar pocket and the entire Seventh Army could have been cut off.[137]

The two divisions organized late in the process were living examples of ill training. The 63rd and 70th Divisions activated in 1943 were among the last to be organized and equipped by the army and both divisions were scheduled to be trained according to the same standard training plan that the 79th, 100th and 103rd had gone through.

Instead, both divisions were used to provide replacements to divisions already in combat. The 63rd Division had only half of its authorized strength as late as 1944. Both divisions had been stripped of junior enlisted soldiers to provide replacements to units already in combat. The 63rd lost 3,200 men in February and 4,185 (3,568 infantry) between April and September 1944. The 70th lost 3,000 men in February and 3,370 (2845 infantry) by September 1944.[138]

Some other factors made the situation even worse. Neither division went through the twelve-week large-scale maneuvers in their training process. Each division lost valuable opportunities for the units to train together.

The 63rd division arrived in the ETO in December 1944 without their artillery, and their individual regiments were assigned to veteran divisions in the VI and XV Corps.

The army is to be commended for sending the three unprepared divisions overseas in November and December 1944. The battle situation was so critical that these divisions made the difference in holding the line against the Nordwind attack.

---

[137] Whiting 112
[138] Bonn 175, 178-179

The German army mobilized divisions in the 1940s with men coming from one area. The unit cohesion in the German army was initially strong—until disasters occurred on both the eastern and western fronts. For example, Wolf T. Zoepf in *"Seven Days in January"* stated that he and his sergeant were together from June 1942 until the sergeant was killed in January 1945 in Alsace.

The German army formed Volks-Grenadier divisions out of broken divisions from the eastern front, students, airmen and other stragglers. Time did not permit adequate training or staffing with officers. Each regiment had two battalions, commanded by captains or lieutenants, which meant there was no reserve. The result of six years of war meant they were very short of officers.[139]

The two battalions from the 313th and 314th effectively stopped the German attack at Reipertswiller. There can be little question that the quick and decisive reaction of the US command to the onslaught of Nordwind was the major factor in the results of the second day of Nordwind. Generals Patch, Brooks and Haislip quickly shuffled divisions in the northeast sector of VI Corps to the endangered sectors during the night of January 1st, 1945.

In executing the shifting of divisions, Lieutenant General Brooks had little choice but to burden General Fredericks with the command of the 45th Division, which had more than twenty-six infantry battalions and ten artillery battalions. The line was twenty-two kilometers long but, with the main line of resistance, was twice that distance.[140]

The complete absence of the German Luftwaffe permitted major movements of American troops on roads within the VI

---

[139] Zoepf 136
[140] Zoepf 176

Corps sector during the daytime. American troops were trucked out over 100 killometers overnight to plug the holes in the line.[141]

The German army lacked the "walkie-talkie" equipment possessed by the American army. The development of two-way radio technology in Germany was retarded in the 1930s by a ban on amateur radio communications since, as they were coming to power, the Nazis feared an opposition group would use radios against them.

Each German army corps had large communications trucks to communicate with divisions and other units. This tenuous situation was made worse by the loss of much of the LXXXIX Corps' communications equipment in the rout at the Saverne Pass. This loss hampered the command to a great degree in the next two months due to the rugged terrain over which the corps would fight, and its wide sector (about 56 km). This was an especially serious shortcoming, because radio delays and a vast quantity of field wire would be essential for command control.[142]

In *"Seven Days in January"* Wolf T. Zoepf describes the problems with the loss of communications equipment. Five-hour delays occurred in evaluating the plan, formulating an alternate, sending a messenger by foot over snow-drifted mountains and then the delays in receiving a reply by messenger.

Other problems were caused by breakdowns in communications for corps and division commanders who were deprived of knowledge of current actions. "The lost communication assets were never replaced. (The American army had an abundance of equipment so would have replaced the captured equipment the next day). Obviously, this communications lapse had already had several consequences for our operations (lack of artillery

---

[141] Zoepf 111
[142] Bonn 143

support, no passage of intelligence updates, delay of orders, etc.) and without such contact from the commanding generals there could be neither reinforcements nor assault guns."

General Philippi had to postpone an attack on Reipertswiller for six hours due to absence of communications with his supporting artillery. This delay allowed the 313th Infantry Regiment enough time to organize its defense, which prevented capture by the German army.[143]

The three battalions from the 313th and 314th Regiments served with distinction in repelling the German attack at Reipertswiller from January 3rd to January 14th, 1945. The breakthrough was finally stopped and the Germans driven back. Since the 79th Division was not involved in a direct way I will not cover this story further. For information on Nordwind see Wolf T. Zoepf's *"Seven Days in January,"* Keith E. Bonn's ***"When the Odds were Even"*** and Charles Whiting's ***"America's Forgotten Army."***

GAMBSHEIM ATTACK FROM THE RHINE

The Germans ferried troops across the Rhine River at Gambsheim on the morning of January 5th, 1945 hitting the new 42nd Division (the famed Rainbow Division from World War I).

When General Brooks of the VI Corps heard of the attack at Gambsheim, he ordered General Wyche of the 79th Division to get in there and get it cleaned up. General Wyche had to telephone Brooks to explain that with the 42nd's state of training, the fight around Gambsheim was going badly. The 79th was heavily involved in Wissembourg.[144]

---

[143] Zoepf 108
[144] Weigley 555

On January 7, 1945 Colonel Luck of the 21ˢᵗ Panzer Division approached the Maginot Line south of Wissembourg at Rittershoffen as told by Stephen Ambrose in *"Citizen Soldier."*

> *"Suddenly we could make out the first bunker, which received us with heavy fire, our leading and the accompanying (self-propelled vehicle) landed in the thick minefield. The artillery stepped up its barrage of fire." Apparently the mines we laid had some effect!"*

American men from 42ⁿᵈ and 79ᵗʰ Divisions used the firing points from pill boxes, retractable cannon, trenches, and other features of the line and stopped the Germans cold.[145] The battle for Hatten and Rittershoffen was an eleven-day bloody affair, which saw two battalions of the 315ᵗʰ Infantry hold these two small Maginot Line towns against two elite German divisions.

Colonel Luck, a veteran of Poland, France, Russia, North Africa and Normandy, characterized the battle as one of the hardest and most costly battles that he had experienced. Both sides fired their artillery almost nonstop at 10,000 rounds each day. The lines were never more than one or two streets apart and sometimes the Germans were in one floor and the Americans in another floor. Flamethrowers were used to set houses on fire, adding to the horror, especially for the civilian population hiding in basements.[146]

What greatly impressed Wolf T. Zoepf from the first contact with American troops was their tendency and their capability to use artillery to break German resistance before committing infantry. In the eyes of the Germans, the Americans seemed to have no real shortage of mortar or artillery ammunition (a point with which many American commanders in the

---

[145] Ambrose, Citizen Solders 386
[146] Ambrose, Citizen Solders 387

heat of battle in Europe would disagree). Only when they believed an objective had been shelled and neutralized would the infantry be sent to take the objective.[147]

The Lorraine Cross newspaper of July 3, 1945 contained an article on a twenty-nine year old Wehrmacht major held prisoner by the 79th Division. Major Kurz of the 21st Panzer Division in tangling with the 315th in the Battle of Rittershoffen stated when questioned, "I never thought much of the Americans as soldiers until I fought them at Rittershoffen. But there we found an antagonist who defended bitterly and with more determination than we had previously seen Americans demonstrate."

The 21st Panzer Grenadier Division Artillery had assault units supported by six self-propelled guns, a large number of tanks, including flame-throwing tanks, eight new flak trucks mounting the deadly triple barrel .37mm guns, and supporting artillery in excess of eight battalions. The infantry battalions had .80mm and .120mm mortars, while American mortars were confined to .60mm and .81mm.

Major Kurz recalled that, on the night of January 13th, two flame-throwing tanks and forty infantrymen made a direct attack on the pillboxes of the 315th. The attack failed when one tank was knocked out and another threw a track leaving the Germans little alternative but retreat in a hail of small arms and automatic weapons fire.[148]

The 315th Regiment was supported by the negro 827th Tank Destroyer Battalion and tanks and armor from the 14th Armored Division.

---

[147] Zoepf 214
[148] Lorraine Cross Vol 1 no. 5 July 3, 1945

ICE STORM

Along with the snow came a severe ice storm. Evidently the army had no snowplows or sanding equipment, so we loaded gravel on our $2\frac{1}{2}$-ton dump truck and spread the gravel for a mile or two shovel by shovel. (see picture in 79th History p. 104)

To clear the roads after a deep snow, we fashioned a homemade plow from steel beams in a triangle, and a large steel plate for the plow. Six of us sat on top of the plow to give it weight. The cold and blowing snow was almost unbearable when the plow moved with any kind of speed. Most of us had frozen faces and lips—in fact, to this day I have a lip problem that requires lip balm 5 or 6 times a day.

In January 1945 the ground was frozen and snow-covered. The infantry needed help in digging foxholes. We supplied the 313th companies with blocks of TNT to blow holes which aided the digging.

ROADBLOCKS

Army intelligence warned each division that German troops dressed as Americans and driving American jeeps might try to sneak through our lines. We challenged each vehicle by asking the password. The dangerous part came when we pulled a string of mines across the road. When the vehicles did not see us in the dark and did not hear us, they came to a screeching halt. We stopped after one night of having freezing butts and feet.

At the height of the Nordwind battle, the 7th Army was concerned about a breakthrough comparable in scope to the Battle of The Bulge (see discussion of Nordwind earlier in this chapter).

PFCs Pokoy and Pal were assigned the job of wiring a bridge with forty lbs. of TNT, then wait until the last vehicle crossed to blow the bridge. Forty or fifty tanks of the 12th Armored were spread out in a field. We could hear and see them firing their guns.

Pokoy placed the TNT on the steel beams standing on a 5' stepladder. When he was hooking up the fuse and igniter, an 88mm shell hit the bridge, killing Pokoy instantly. In yet another miracle, what are the odds of a shell exploding within five feet of forty lbs. of TNT without exploding or harming PFC Pal, standing less than five feet below? I pulled Pokoy out of the water and determined he was dead before I left to watch from a nearby house. It was bitterly cold with drifting and blowing snow.

As I was watching, I saw an old man walking in a trance-like state carrying an infant by the arm that had been hit by a shell, and so was bloody and missing a leg. Relief came in an hour or two. The 12th Armored Division stopped the Germans so the bridge was not blown.

I forgot this incident until January 1983 when we were driving from Falls Church, Virginia to our vacation home in West Virginia. Solveig, our oldest granddaughter, was in her car seat. It was a cold, snowy night. When we got to Hillsboro, the traffic was stopped waiting behind a snowplow; all of a sudden I was back in Alsace with tanks coming up the road (flashback number six).

January 16th to 19th witnessed three days and nights of savage fighting in Hatten and Rittershoffen. Barrage after barrage of artillery, mortar, and tank fire, hit the GIs in both towns. More than ten attacks were stopped before any real penetration could be made. Finally on January 19th, the Germans made the largest and most concentrated attack on Hatten. After a ninety-minute artillery barrage of more than 3,000 rounds, the battle raged for two hours with the 315th holding on with no loss of ground. This bitter battle earned presidential citations for three battalions of the 79th Division.[149]

For its part in helping repulse the Germans' frantic struggle to break out in Alsace, the battalion was awarded a presidential citation. This citation was the only one given to a non-infantry unit.

The 310th Field Artillery Battalion was cited for extraordinary and outstanding performance of duty against the enemy in the defense of Rittershoffen and Hatten. The citation reads:

> *"Repulsing almost continuous enemy attacks by a thunderous volume of fire, this inspired battalion rendered unusually effective support to friendly infantry for a period of twelve days; interdicted and harassed enemy supply routes, communication centers, and assembly areas, and greatly aided in the dispersal of attempts by enemy armor and infantry units to overrun the sector and to effect a decisive breakthrough.*

> *"Despite adverse weather conditions, the mission of supporting four widely dispersed infantry battalions and the coordination of the fires of eight additional field artillery battalions; all duties were performed un-hesitatingly each success fire mission called for.*

> *"The performance of all members of the battalion, the number of missions fired and the effectiveness of all support fires over an extended period of time, were such as to distinguish this battalion above all other artillery battalions which participated in the same action. This*

---

[149] History of the 79th 106

gallantry, professional skill, and initiative exhibited by the 310th Field Artillery Battalion contributed directly to repulsing of repeated fanatical enemy attacks and will be forever in the annals of warfare."[150]

A German soldier, interrogated by my friend Rudy Thell, said American artillery is so horrible that a man's hair can turn grey overnight. Rudy Thell spoke German, so he was asked to interrogate German prisoners captured by A Company 304th Engineers.

Colonel Porter borrowed thirty-five volunteer riflemen from Company A 304th Engineers Battalion. These volunteers were never needed. One part of the enemy attack in company strength struck Company K and retired under concentrated rifle and automatic fire and artillery support. Minutes later, German infantry, moving in front of the tanks, attacked Company K again. The white-clad Germans were driven back, but the tanks kept coming into a minefield fronting the area. The minefield laid by Company A 304th Engineers Battalion claimed at least two tanks. One tank had its tread blown off and the remaining tanks retreated.

The Germans struck again for a third time and the determined battalion turned them back. The supporting artillery worked with almost perfect efficiency. Destroying two tanks, Colonel Porter recalled that one minute the tanks were there, firing to beat hell, the next second they were plain missing—the Germans were forced to withdraw for the last time.

During the eleven-day battle, enemy aircraft were very active, bombing and strafing small towns and main roads in the rear of the division front. Many of the sorties were carried

---

[150] Lorraine Cross—Weekly Paper of 79th Vol 1 No 4, June 29 1945

out by the new jet-propelled ME-262. The plane was so fast that it was difficult to see, but you could hear the roar is it went over. On January 13th, the 463rd Anti-Aircraft Battalion had the honor of being the first AA Battalion in the ETO to officially down a jet plane (see Appendix).[151]

On January 21, 1945 General Patch ordered the 79th and 14th Armored Divisions to retreat from Rittershoffen to a new line on the Moder River. The defensive line included the three 79th regiments and two regiments of the 42nd Division. For the next five days patrolling and raiding parties received the top priority.

The 313th Infantry needed to capture prisoners to discover the extent of preparations for a pre-attack buildup. Company A 304th Engineers was given the task of constructing two log footbridges for an infantry company to cross over and the third platoon did the work. We found four logs about 12" thick which were spread about 24" apart and then boards were nailed for treads. Ten men carried each bridge.

The artillery started at 8:55 p.m. After the barrage, we started carrying the bridges over a cold, snow-covered landscape. After about 200 yards or so, we came to concertina barbed wire. We cut a path through the barbed wire, when several star flares illuminated the area. We dropped to the ground, when six 120mm mortar shells came down within twenty or thirty feet of us. To our amazement, all six were duds and one came so close that I felt the dirt raised by the shell. I don't remember whether I helped carry the bridge or not, but the bridges were put in place. By 11:30 the infantry company captured four prisoners who provided the needed information.[152] Sergeant Willis Nale received a Bronze Star for leading the platoon.

---

[151] History of the 79th 101
[152] History of the 313th 155

In 1999, when watching the movie, *Schindler's List,* I thanked the Jews who sabotaged these shells.

Stephen Ambrose in *"Citizen Soldiers"* described the duds phenomena as follows:

> *"...over four decades of interviewing former GIs, I've been struck by how often they tell stories about duds, generally shells falling near their foxholes and failing to explode...there are no statistics available on this phenomenon, nor is there no evidence on why, but I've never heard a German talk about American duds. The shells fired by the GIs were made by free American labor; the shells fired by the Wehrmacht were made by slave labor from Poland, France and throughout the German empire, and at least some of the slaves must have mastered the art of turning out shells that passed examination but where nevertheless sabotaged effectively."* [153]

Overall, the Nordwind offensive was an extreme failure. They never got to Strasbourg, nor were they able to break out through the Saverne Gap. The battle was expensive for both sides; Seventh Army's losses in January 1945 were 11,609 plus 2,836 cases of trench foot and 380 cases of frostbite. German losses were estimated at 23,000 killed, wounded or missing and with 6,000 prisoners of war.

The US Army's well-trained formations had the potential to win in difficult circumstances against almost any threat. As the war came close to German borders, the Wehrmacht fielded units organized without the means to meet the enemy threat on numerically equal terms, or on terrain of its own choosing.

Colonel Hans von Luck, who commanded units in combat against the French, Russians and British before leading his regiment in the 21st Panzer Division against the Seventh Army

---

[153] Ambrose, Citizen Solders 65,66

in the Vosges, stated his opinion of the American forces.

"In one respect, they seemed to have the edge over their British allies; they were extraordinarily flexible. They adapted immediately to a changed condition and fought with great doggedness...we discovered later, in Italy, and I personally in the battles in France in 1944, how quickly the Americans were able to evaluate their experience and through flexible and unconventional conduct of a battle, convert it into results."[154]

He might have added that these results were received when the odds were even.[155]

The good news that we were to be relieved by the 101st Airborne Division came on February 5th, 1945. The 79th was to move to Pont-a-Mousson for two weeks rest after eighty-seven days of continuous combat and a total of 213 days of combat since June 19, 1944.

We jumped into our $2\frac{1}{2}$ -ton truck at sundown on a very cold February winter's day. I crawled on top of the duffle bags and sprawled out the best way I could on the pile. The canvas top and end flap were down, so we should have been relatively comfortable but the kitchen served beans and other gas-producing foods, and several men ate large cloves of garlic. The results were predictable, but amid much complaining, shouting and laughing we arrived at our destination early in the morning.

For two days we rested, with each man doing exactly as he chose to do. After the two-day rest, we started to clean our equipment, including rifles, axes, picks, shovels, saws, heavy equipment, etc. Training, close order drills, were mixed in with leave to tour the city. We also got to enjoy movies and beer

---

[154] Von Luck 142
[155] Bonn 230, 231

parties. I was interested in World War I and the city of Pont-a-Mousson. What I discovered there I have forgotten long ago, but I still have some post cards.

We stayed in an old French barracks in a city that was near the front for much of World War I. We were now away from artillery fire and for a period of time, no foxholes. We took our fourth shower since May 30th, 1944, and received new clean clothing.

THE OFFICERS' MESS

One day during our rest period, an announcement was made setting up an eating area for the officers. One enlisted man was to put the meal on plates and then serve the officers around the tables. He would also set the table with silverware, water glasses, and coffee and tea. When I heard these instructions, I sought out Lt. Macrino to warn him of the ill will that this move would cause. He told me that the decision had already been made so any appeal on my part was futile.

Since the establishment of the 304th Engineers Battalion in 1942, the relations between officers and enlisted men had been very good. The officers and men had grown up together through maneuvers and into combat. The relationship in combat was on a friendly basis, where we often discussed the options before taking action. The officers' lives were really no different than the mens' lives in combat conditions. The only difference usually was a better uniform and gold or silver bars on their helmets. The enlisted men often remarked, "It didn't take an act of Congress to make us gentlemen."

The decision to have separate dining areas and use combat men as waiters hit everyone very hard, with the disappointment showing in voices and curses. The general opinion of the men was that the system would last one day only at the most.

The man selected to serve as a waiter was bitter about it, as he thought this was a waste of a perfectly good combat engineer. He showed this displeasure by mixing their food together and slinging the plates on the table. We were all pleased to see the bulletin board notice that discontinued the officers' mess.

WORSHIP

One day during our two-week break, the first sergeant introduced the new chaplain, a Baptist. The new chaplain asked the first sergeant to get the men to come to church. This was a big surprise, as the battalion had not had church since the service in Alsace in November, 1944. The platoon sergeants announced that everyone was encouraged to go, and as a result over 100 men came to hear the new chaplain. He stood up and led an old-fashioned hymn sing. The men, most of them from the south, were familiar with the Southern Baptist service, and clapped hands and sang along to the gospel songs with great gusto. He started midweek Bible study groups. In fact, I read the lessons for Holy Week and also made some comments before the chaplain took over the discussion. These well-attended services lasted until the day we left the area.

15

To the Rhine River

O n February 17th we were ready to travel again to an unknown destination. A rumor made the rounds that we were joining Ninth Army, which would have meant that we'd made all of them: the First, the Third, the Seventh, and if the rumors proved to be true, now the Ninth.

We started early in the morning and by midnight pulled into an area north of Tongres, Belgium.[156] We stayed in the Tongres area until February 22nd, when we got into trucks for a move to Heerlen, Holland. Heerlen (or Herrleheid) is a coal mining area in the province of Lemburg in a narrow neck of land between Germany and Holland.

On February 23rd, the 314th and division artillery were to clear the west bank and relieve the 35th Division. This campaign lasted until February 28th when the 314th rejoined the 79th Division.[157]

By early March the Ninth Army was clearing out the west bank of the Rhine and looking for a bridge that was still standing. Although they found no bridges standing, General Simpson (considered by many to be the soundest of the army commanders in strategy, planning, and execution) requested permission to cross at Urdinger, where the Germans had only

---

[156] History of the 313th 157
[157] History of the 79th 113

a few troops. Simpson thought the open terrain of the northern side of the Ruhr Valley offered considerable potential for exploitation. The 79th and 30th Divisions would have been selected for this task. General Montgomery turned Simpson down cold, in order to wait for three weeks for his own "massive, ponderous, carefully planned and executed and long advertised" crossing of the Rhine to take place. According to Murray and Millett in *"A War to be Won,"* this indicated why General Montgomery was unsuited for the position of overall Allied Commander of Ground Forces.[158]

Since the early crossing of the Rhine was not allowed, we went back to life in Heerlen with a Dutch family that had taken us in earlier. The infantry regiments all had an extensive training regimen, but Company A had only briefings until the big day. We enjoyed life in the spring days, including a trip to Maastrich. I still have some post cards.

Company A was assigned to cross with the Second Battalion of the 313th. On D-Minus-1 we were trucked halfway, then walked the remaining six miles, moving into an old brick kiln to wait for the artillery to start. Before the artillery started, we watched the U.S. bombers destroying Essen, the flames from the resulting firestorm rose several thousand feet. It was a spectacular display, but I was sobered to think of the thousands of innocent German civilians burned to death, a thought which I am sure was not shared by my mates in Company A.

General Montgomery's attack across the Rhine rivaled the Normandy invasion in terms of the scope of the large force and buildup behind it—three armies of thirty divisions, six armored and two airborne. He also had five thousand artillery guns; the British had sixty thousand tons of ammunition, thirty

---

[158] Murray & Millett 477

thousand tons of engineering equipment and the Royal Navy would provide the landing craft. General Montgomery and Winston Churchill crossed the Rhine in a 79th Division assault boat.

At H-minus-1 the artillery of the fifty battalions started. The fire was so heavy that the reports of individual guns were blended into one solid roar. The gun flashes kept the sky in a blaze of light and the whistle of thousands of shells overhead sounded like freight trains. The bursting shells seemed to cover the far shore.[159]

General Eisenhower joined General Simpson in a church tower to watch the artillery barrage because the batteries were distributed on the flat plains on the western bank of the Rhine. The Supreme Commander reported that every flash could be seen. For sixty minutes, more than a thousand shells a minute crossed the Rhine, 65,261 rounds in all. At the same time, 1,406 Eighth Air Force B-17s and B-24s were attacking Luftwaffe bases just to the east.[160] I fell asleep during the bombardment. The noise lulled me to sleep, so I kept my record of the only man to sleep through extreme noise.

The hour-long preparation finally ended. I couldn't believe anyone could possibly have survived on the other side of the river. After a walk of ½ mile, we joined the line to get in the assault boat. Our turn came and as we jumped in the boat, shells fell nearby. The Navy man operating the boat cursed at the bad luck. He said he had had enough of being shelled.

As we crossed the Rhine, the far side was almost completely enshrouded in smoke and fog. We saw men in the fog that looked like ghosts. Craters were everywhere and dead bodies

---

[159] History of the 313th 161, 162
[160] Weigley 645

were in evidence. Some of the Germans were still dazed from the artillery fire. At dawn, a smoke-generating unit covered the river flank of the division. The 42mm mortars fired white phosphorous shells to hide the operation. It also devastated the German units and made the entire area uninhabitable.

The first squad fumbled our way until we came to the town of Walsum. Sergeant Nale picked out a house and everybody dashed in to select a room. All the rooms were taken on the first floor, so I picked an upstairs bedroom, which had only one problem: the red tile roof had sections open to the sky. I laid down for a nap when shells came in. I heard the men around me running for cover, but I stayed in bed, as I didn't think the shells were close enough to hurt me.

16

The End of the Fighting

The next day the infantry was on the move into the Ruhr Valley, the heart of German industry, without much opposition. The First and Ninth Armies were cutting off the Ruhr Valley, encircling nearly three hundred thousand German troops.

TWO HUNDRED BOTTLES OF SWEET VERMOUTH

The first large industrial city in the Ruhr was Hamborn. Huge areas of the city were destroyed while in other areas, the lights were on and things functioned normally. Company A was assigned a large apartment building for a residence for several nights. After selecting apartments to sleep in, some of the men went exploring. One or two found the cellar, which contained over 200 quarts of sweet Vermouth. They distributed a quart to any man who wanted one. Personally, I believe that sweet Vermouth is the worst liquor to drink if you drink a lot. Within an hour or so, many of them had become very drunk or sick. I had trouble finding six sober men to stand guard that night.

SIX CORPSES

Two men came into an apartment, only to see some draped figures on a large table. They pulled the sheets away to find six dead, naked bodies. They departed the apartment in record time.

The next move was to the city of Horst, about twelve kilometers from Hamborn. The mission of the 79th was to cross the Rhine-Herne Canal. The Rhine Herne Canal is a double canal at the place chosen for the crossing. It was thirty-five yards wide with perpendicular walled sides, about twenty feet high. Company A was given the task of laying a footbridge. This was quite a task to get the bridging equipment down the steep sides and across the canal. We were shelled periodically, but finally got the footbridge laid.

On April 8, the 79th captured its 25,000th prisoner, a Corporal Schmidt of 2nd Parachute Division who had been in the German army since 1941.

From April 8th to 11th, the division captured cities Bochum, Essen, and Gelsenkirchen. We captured the famous Alfred Krupp of the vast steel munitions empire. As we stood in the absolute ruins of the Krupp and Thyssen factories, I thought of how the might behind the German war machine had ended in rubble.

Standing there viewing the vast devastation, I had a feeling of evil still there from the Nazi leadership that resulted in millions of dead. I recalled Paul's statement in Ephesians 6:12 *"For we wrestle not against flesh and blood, but against principalities, against powers, against the rulers of darkness of this world, against spiritual wickedness, in high places."*

On April 14th, our division met the 8th Infantry and closed the loop encircling the Germans in the net. The period of April 14th – 30th was spent in policing the area assigned, we were to provide military government detachments in Dortmund, Hulls, Westerholt and others.

RHINE TO V.E. DAY

On April 18th, 1945, the 79th Infantry Division received a letter from commanding General Simpson as follows:

"Assignment of the 79th Infantry Division to the Ninth Army afforded me great pleasure, inasmuch as I had noted with keen interests the fine record made by the division since operations were launched on the continent.

It was a feeling of complete confidence that your division was chosen as one of two assault units for the initial Rhine crossing in the Ninth Army Zone.

I particularly wish to commend your Division upon the skill and speed with which you accomplished the crossing, in the face of determined opposition and numerous difficulties. Beyond your control equally impressive we were the rapidity with which you built up your strength on the far shore, and the energy and power with which you exploited the initial bridgehead."[161]

Lt. General W.H. Simpson
Commanding, Ninth U.S. Army
April 18, 1945

---

[161] History of the 79th 133

BLOWN OUT MOUNTAIN ROAD

The Germans almost completely blew out a mountain road back to the solid rock cliff. We were asked if we could restore the road within five days.

We placed extension rods on the jackhammer and started drilling into the rocks with the jackhammers about chest high. When we had completed four or five holes we packed each hole with Composition C, an explosive that resembles modeling clay. The resulting explosion loosened a great deal of rock. These explosions and the resulting rock, repeated many times, produced enough rock which, when combined with truckloads of fill dirt, combined to produce a passable road up the mountainside.

TIGER TANK

On one of the last days of war, the first squad received an order to pull mines from the middle of a road. We arrived at the scene on a dark night. We found burning buildings lighting the entire area. The mines were pointed out to us and we entered the street to remove the mines. A Tiger tank fired at us from almost point-blank range with their 88mm gun, often considered the best weapon of the war. Fortunately for us the round missed us. Twenty minutes later we tried again with the same results, although this time the 88mm gun came closer. The conversation turned to the fact that we had gotten through the war intact, only to be at risk of death on one of the last nights of the war. After one more try, we gave up and advised the infantry officers that it was not possible to do the job under direct fire.

On May 8, we were in a quaint town of Arnsburg, in the Black Forest. The dinner of VE day was served with table clothes, china, spoons, knives and forks, and wine was also served (during combat, we only ate with a spoon). The mood was jubilant but at the same time there was a sober sense of all we had gone through and the remembrance of men that were no longer with us.

Charles Whiting, in *America's Forgotten Army,* described the VE day experience as follows:

"Now it was over at last."

"Some got drunk on that first day of peace in Europe. Some wandered around in a daze, puzzled by the strange loud silence now that the guns no longer rumbled. Many couldn't believe it. They had longed for peace for months and years. Then suddenly, it was upon them all and the impact of the fact was a thing that failed register—like the sudden death of a loved one."

—wrote the fabled historian of the 3rd Division.[162]

DISPLACED PERSONS

Hitler was determined that the German people should not feel the effects of the war. They were to have everything they needed, and with the conquest of much of Europe with all its human and mineral riches, in greater abundance than ever before.

Albert Speer opposed this easy option. He advised Hitler that total war required sacrifice and discipline, from all Germans, male or female. Speer tried to influence German officials with the need to recruit labor from the large pool of German women. The leaders, Goering and Fritz Sauchel and Borman, lobbied against using German women as an offense

---

[162] Whiting 197

against the sacred nature of German womanhood and that factory work could be morally harmful to German women.

Fritz Sauchel, Gauleiter of Munich, informed Speer, the Production Czar of Germany, of Hitler's decision to bring into the Reich from the eastern territories between 400,000 and 500,000 carefully selected healthy and strong girls. These decisions had fateful consequences later in the war.[163]

After the war Germany was severely criticized for two major things: the extermination of Jews and for mistreating a million displaced persons in camps working for German industry. The sad part was that when most of these displaced persons and POWs returned to the Soviet Union, Stalin had them exiled to Siberia or killed. None of this would have happened if they had used German women in industry. See Chapter 14 for the shells produced by slave labor, which included many duds.

DP CAMPS

The 79th Division was assigned eighteen displaced persons camps to run. These camps took many forms, from modern barracks, schoolhouses, to airports. The nationalities represented Russia and nearly the entirety of eastern Europe, including Poland, Latvia, Estonia, Ukraine, Yugoslavia, Czechoslovakia, as well as French, Italian, and Dutch POWs. The logistics of moving thousands of half starving, wild-eyed men, women and children, who spoke any of a dozen languages, was a daunting, terrific job. They were united in only one thing—their hatred of the Germans and to take revenge for their misery.

Policing of the ordinary German was not difficult, since the German army (and much of Germany) had largely been

---

[163] Sereny 311

destroyed and they recognized that the Americans were their only protection from their former slaves.[164]

The 304th Engineers Battalion took charge of a camp located in a large former German barracks. We were greeted by a large number of half-starved displaced people and Russian POWs.

Just before we arrived a group of men from the camp had escaped and terrorized the neighborhood surrounding the camp. They killed a cow or two, which were used by the Americans to feed the starving Germans.

Our first task was to determine the family units. One member from each family was to pick up their family's portions. The cooks started to prepare a meal of meat (that smelled bad) cut up into sauerkraut.

I guarded the chow line. Each person would report on the number of people in the group and the cooks would ladle the required number of cups. The smell in the chow line reminded me of when my mother would boil meat for dog scraps. The people in the line were happy to have food, though, as many had not eaten in the days since the air raids destroyed the German industry.

The line formed was comprised of mostly men; when some of them got unruly I would have to club them with a rifle butt. We had no further trouble in the chow line. The war changes men into hardy strong things.

The next morning I found vomit all over the floor and the stairway. Moving on, I discovered the urinals and toilets filled with urine, waste and potato peels. Evidently the displaced persons had never used flushing toilets. I selected two Russian POWs and started the cleanup of the urinals. One of them

---

[164] History of the 313th 168

balked at cleaning the urinals with their hands. After a bit of threats and shouting on my part, the job was finished, and they were rewarded with cigarettes and a candy bar. I then made the rounds, inspecting the rooms in my area. People were assigned to rooms without regard to sex or age. To my surprise every room was in good order. I felt sorry for the people who had lost all personal privacy.

The bathrooms were a mess for three days and then they caught on how to flush urinals and toilets. I also got to know people in each room, which made for pleasant relationships. My friend Buck also got involved with his people. One day he invited me into one of the rooms that he oversaw. We were greeted warmly, and then a lady brought out some fried pork patties and a cup. I ate the meatball and the drink, which turned out to be Buzz Bomb Juice (190 proof alcohol). After one drink, I put the cup down and thanked the lady for her kindness.

After a week or so we moved on with the 79th Division. I don't remember who took over the DP camp but the 101st Airborne or local civil government took it over.

CARS, CARS AND MORE CARS

During late April and early May, when our lives as combat engineers were over, one main interest was collecting abandoned cars on the street. The collection grew to eight or nine cars running around. The best one was a Mercedes staff car comparable to Hitler's limo. To keep the cars running the men used gasoline cans they found in the motor pool area. The end came when we were ordered to turn in the acquired cars; but rather than turn in the Mercedes, they ran it into a tree and smashed the front end.

NON-FRATERNIZATION POLICY

The policy instructed the American soldier to have no social relationships with the German civilian population. Most GIs did not take this restriction very seriously-even with the threat of courts martial.

We were housed in an apartment building with a large courtyard. We were using nails and evidently some spilled on the ground. A German man's horse stepped on a nail, and he had stopped to bathe the wound in a Lysol solution. A T/Sgt Eppler was speaking to the man in German. About a half-dozen of us were standing around watching, when Lieutenant Colonel Van Allen and First Lieutenant Warga came into view. Lt. Colonel Van Allen started to yell at us to disburse and that we all would be court-martialed for fraternizing with Germans. We all scattered except for Sgt. Eppler who was reduced in rank to a private. First Lieutenant Warga told Van Allen that he did not recognize any of us.

Many of the men shared their food, cigarettes and candy with the German people. They gave them canned goods stolen from the kitchen etc. Most of the men had no hard feelings for German people and in fact were concerned for their lack of food and shelter.

One day, the officers advised that we were to search the Germans' houses and apartments. We barged into houses and made a thorough search. We took back all the items given to the Germans. We stood watching this with a feeling of regret of being Indian givers to starving people.

The army gave this policy of non-fraternization up as counter-productive after a few weeks. We were approached by any number of children asking for food and candy. A little German girl approached me with the standard lingo for a girl her age, telling me that for five years she had had no chocolate or meat, only potato soup and black bread. I asked her how old she was, and she replied in German that she was only five years old.

FRATERNIZATION IN THE MOONLIGHT

By V.E. day PFC Oldham recovered from his illness and came back to Company A. He was a thin man from Kansas City, Missouri, who thought he was really something special. He would tie his scarf around his neck and primp his hair to make himself attractive to the women. He found another friend just like himself, and these two would go out almost every night with German women. He told me they had sex two or three times a night. After a couple weeks he failed "short arm" inspection since his penis dripped. The doctors also noticed teeth marks on his penis, so they asked him loud enough for others to hear of his "battle scars." Later the doctors advised him that he had damaged his prostate gland and would have to give up sex and alcohol for at least six months or he would be sterile for life. He then went to the hospital, never to be seen or heard from again. I tried to locate him in Kansas City but was unable to reach him.

MUSIC BY WAGNER

In the last week of the war, the German radio played somber music by Wagner much of the day, with little or no speaking in between records. The days seem to all fall into a rhythm of a dark, smoky haze as we witnessed the death of Hitler's Germany. This great empire that tried to rule the world was now reduced to rubble and ashes, with many widows and homeless children trying to survive on 500 calories a day. I shared a feeling of melancholy over this great tragedy in the lives of millions of poor people that were not responsible for the horror that they were going through.

I was elated that the war was over in Europe, but at the same time sorry for the state of suffering in Germany. The battles were costly to the men in the 79th Division. In 248 days of combat the division suffered 14,875 battle casualties and 8,582 non-battle casualties (including trenchfoot, accidents, sickness, and battle fatigue) for a total of 23,457 for a turnover rate of 166.5%.[165]

Most of the men got back to civilian life without too many problems. But some would feel the effects of the conflict all the days of their lives. There was V.E. day but no peace within for these warriors. I heard the artillery in my sleep for years, and still occasionally experience flashbacks.

But one day after V.E. day, everything was back to normal. Close order drills, formations, parades. The army was getting back to soldiering once more.[166]

---

[165] Ambrose, Citizen Solders 281
[166] Whiting 198

17

Sudetenland

On June 16th, 1945, the division was sent to the Sudetenland along the western border of Czechoslovakia, to block the advance of the Russian army. The trip was made in two days, through the Danube River and mountain scenery of the Bavarian Alps. We landed in a quaint town of FranzJosefsbad. It seemed good to stay in a city with no war damage. We stayed in a large, well-maintained house. A park was nearby where we watched a German band play on the weekends. Their famous mineral baths were open but none of us went due to the rundown condition of the buildings.

A few days later we took our trucks to the large city of Pilsen (now Cheb). We saw the roadblocks set up by the 313th Infantry to mark the U.S. zone from the Russian zone. Company A stayed at an airbase in an old German barracks. One of the favorite pastimes was to shoot out the glass insulators that hold up the lines. One afternoon, we shot out so many insulators that the power line came down. Needless to say, that put a stop to the shooting. (In 2003, a news item from Iraq reported soldiers bringing down power lines. Good sport for bored soldiers has not changed from World War II to today.)

At night we slept on tables. After an hour or so, I could feel the bites of bed bugs, eventually causing my fingers to become bloody. Fortunately, we only stayed for two nights before returning to FranzJosefsbad.

Jack Benny's troops performed in Marienbad. Several truckloads of us arrived early enough to get good seats. The officers sat in the front rows that were set up thirty – forty feet back from the stage. Benny opened the show by asking the enlisted men to come to the front. I ran with the others and found myself in the front row.

The performers included Benny, Ingrid Berman, Martha Tilton, and Larry Adler. Benny opened with jokes and his fine violin playing. Martha Tilton sang hits of the day. Larry Adler played his many harmonicas. Ingrid Bergman closed the show, wearing a black dress with pearls as the only decoration. She read from the play *Joan of Arc* and brought down the house. At intermission I chatted with Martha Tilton, who said she was worn out from all the travel but very proud to be performing for the fighting men.

First Lieutenant Warga, a true kid at heart, found a glider in good condition, and also found an abandoned airstrip. Six of us spent the rest of the afternoon trying to get the glider to fly. We used a jeep to pull the glider. We got it airborne once, only to see it crash. First Lieutenant Warga was unhurt, but the glider was a wreck. Most of us thought this detail was a misuse of enlisted men's time but no one dared to complain to the company commander in person.

The division soon received notice that we were now in Category II, which meant we would be part of the attack force on Japan. I was named the company dispatcher, which meant that I controlled trucks, jeeps, etc. This assignment lasted only a few weeks before my trip to England.

SCHOOL IN ENGLAND

The Army set up two colleges for the GIs to attend; one at the Sorbonne in Paris and one in Shrivenham, England.

A notice came advising everyone that the 79th had eight slots in the college and that they were requesting applications. I sent a request to attend the college in England. I found out later that I was the only applicant, so notice eventually came that I was accepted. (The number one goal, of most of the men at the time was to go home at the earliest opportunity.)

The day came to report to the 79th HQ and be taken to the train station. The trip to LaHavre took two days due to detours for blown out bridges and torn up track. I was supposed to have been issued rations for two days. This I discovered at lunchtime when the men broke out K rations. I pretended that I had rations at lunch. At dinnertime one man offered me some of his K rations.

The next day the train stopped at a food stop that met the troop trains. I don't remember what was served but I filled myself to hold me over until the next meal. We went from the train to the Channel ferry. The French were still bitter over the bombing of LaHavre two days after the Germans left.

The cross-Channel trip featured rough choppy seas, but I enjoyed it more than the trip on the LST one year before. We landed at Portsmouth and took a train for Swinden, a large rail hub. We went by bus to Shrivenham, a large village whose only claim to fame is the Shrivenham Barracks. The Barracks were brick buildings used for housing and classrooms. The Barracks received 8,500 Dunkirk survivors.

The Shrivenham Post of September 12, 1945 reported:

"Albert G. Hacker, station-master at the Shrivenham Depot, tells of that day five years ago.

'At one time I can remember five special trains pulling in all jammed with men. They were a pretty sad looking lot, too. Dirty, unshaved, some were being carried while others just limped along.'

Members of the Post Staff of Royal Engineers who were there at the time say, 'The men came in wearing perhaps only an overcoat, a pair of pants, some had no shoes. We used every available facility to house them. Twenty-man rooms held forty; tents were pitched in the fields and extra mess halls served nine meals a day. It was a bad time. The men stayed about a month to reform and then went out for another crack at the Jerries.'"

Shrivenham American University was a university in every respect of almost 4,000 students from all over the US. Army faculty members came from the armed forces, or from American universities. One of my professors was a Captain Bone from the air force and one was a professor from Utah. I don't remember who the third professor was.

Meals were served in a large mess hall. The first day, I started to eat with a spoon (the only utensil we used under combat conditions). When I noticed other people watching, I put the spoon down and picked up the fork.

I met a young man from the 80th Division named Robert Jablonksi from Chicago. We were buddies for the thirteen weeks at school. We attended two plays at Stratford-on-Avon: *Twelfth Night*, and *She Stoops to Conquer*. We also took one-day trips to Oxford and Cambridge together during our stay.

Our first trip to London was on the first bank holiday since 1939—a holiday comparable to our Labor Day weekend. We noticed every train leaving London was packed like the old displaced persons (DP) trains. People had bicycles and bags. Arriving at Paddington Station we found few people. We took a bus to the Hans Crescent Hotel, a residential hotel for American servicemen. (I found out in 1994 that it had been torn down.) The hotel had a full range of services. We were expected to eat our meals in the cafeteria. They packed lunches if we were not there for lunch.

The event choices for the Saturday were a walking tour or tennis matches at Wimbledon. Since neither one of us had heard about Wimbledon we opted for the walking tour of Hyde Park, Buckingham Palace, and a variety of statues. Our guide commented on the statue of Queen Victoria, that she was a dear queen in the money she cost England for 75 years. He evidently belonged to the Labour party, as he predicted that if the party were to get control they would abolish the monarchy. (An election was held several weeks later, bringing in a Labour government. They found King George VI and family greatly admired from World War II. They also discovered that the king could also give a Labour speech that provided cover in the country.)

We got tickets through the hotel to see Gay Rosalinda with music by Johann Strauss at the Palace Theatre on August 6th, 1945. We enjoyed the music and dancing.

We also visited Madame Tussauds Exhibition and were amazed at the 344 lifelike wax statues. My friend Bob particularly liked the exhibits in the Chamber of Horrors, appropriately housed in the basement.

That night as we were walking through Piccadilly Circus, a woman approached us clad in a robe. She opened the robe revealing her naked body. She said, "What do you think of these, Yanks? Worth 10 pounds." Since we were two straight soldiers from the Midwest, we ignored her and walked away.

This incident reminded me of Carl Sandberg's poem *Chicago:* "I have seen your women with painted faces standing under street lights luring on the farm boys." Our second trip to London occurred over the celebration Thanksgiving Sunday for the end of WWII. Saturday was spent touring sites such as Runnymede, Windsor Castle, Hampton Court, and Eaton College where we saw the boys dressed in formal wear.

On Sunday afternoon, we stood lined up on the street to watch the royal family, government leaders, and high society come by. I looked at my watch and found that we would have to wait two hours before the procession. I asked Bob, "Do you think the royal family would wait two hours to see us come by?" The answer was no, so we left the parade route and headed for Paddington Station.

As we entered the station, I saw some of the best grapes I had ever seen. I asked the price and was told "a pound a pound," which translated at the time for five U.S. dollars a pound. I obviously didn't buy any grapes.

I received a notice of an awards ceremony on September 12th, only one day away. I went to the barbershop, but the line was too long. I appeared at the ceremony with long hair (the first picture taken of me with long hair). There were nineteen medals awarded (many to officers for managing replacement depots, etc.) There were only five Bronze Stars awarded for heroism. Four infantry divisions were represented, and every one of them was a private or a PFC.

My citation read, in part,

"PFC Philip A. Langehough...distinguished himself by his initiative and devotion to duty while with the 304th Engineers Battalion, 79th Infantry Division" (see Appendix for the complete citation).

Private First Class Philip A. Langehough, 37568495, Corps of
Engineers, 304th Engineer Combat Battalion, United States Army,
for meritorious achievement in action against the enemy from 19
June 1944 to 8 May 1945, in France, Belgium the Netherlands, and
Germany. Throughout this extended period of combat Private
Langehough performed his various engineer duties in a most capable
and efficient manner. Exhibiting unusual ingenuity and sound
judgment in his execution of assigned functions he contributed
greatly to the effective operations of his unit in combat. The
initiative and devotion to duty displayed by Private Langehough
reflect great credit on the armed forces of the United States.
Entered military service from Minnesota.
                                By command of Brigadier General Watson:

OFFICIAL: John A. Gloriod,
    /s/ Odie H. Helton   Colonel, G.S.C.,
    /t/ Odie H. Helton   Chief of Staff.
        Major, A.G.D.,
        Adjutant General.
A TRUE COPY:
        (signed) S. B. Proffitt
                 Major, AGD
                 Adjutant.

The University mailed pictures and the citation to a San Diego paper, which printed it.

Bob and I took a one-day trip to Oxford University. In a letter home, I commented on the number of colleges that made up Oxford. I also wrote that there were 900 women attending separate colleges.

The chaplains held services every day with the largest congregation on Sunday. I attended every Sunday I was on the campus—in fact, I have a bulletin of one Sunday.

The next Sunday we attended a performance of the London Philharmonic Orchestra conducted by Sir Thomas Beecham in Swindon, a concert we really enjoyed. Over the Labor Day weekend, we spent at Bournemouth on the Channel. It rained all weekend, so we spent the time playing ping-pong with the Red Cross girls. Our history class, taught by Capt. Bone traveled to Portsmouth to see Nelson's ship Victory and other sights in the harbor. On the way back we visited the cathedral at Salisbury which is said to be the longest cathedral in England.

The weeks passed quickly and it was soon time to return to Germany to rejoin the 79th Division. We took the train to Portsmouth and got on the Channel ferry to face a rough trip to LeHavre. I spent a day at Camp Lucky Strike (all the replacement centers were named for cigarettes and tobacco companies.) The next day I boarded a train for Germany. The return trip was more enjoyable than its predecessor, as this time I had rations.

RETURN TO GERMANY

According to a letter I wrote to my sister on October 4th, 1945, the train we left LeHavre on was an old 3rd class wooden coach. The trip was Reims, Sedan, Toul, and Mannheim and stopped at Frankfurt. We spent at least twenty-four hours on sidings waiting for faster trains to go through. The waiting continued with a day in Frankfurt waiting on a truck to take me to the 304th Engineers Battalion, now located in Sulzbach. In the morning, Dunham came riding in on a motorcycle*.[167] He offered me a ride but this offer was not as appealing as it sounds—it was a cold October day. Just as I was about to get on the motorcycle a jeep came by to take me to Sulzbach to rejoin A Company.

Sulzbach is a small country town thirty miles from Frankfurt and forty miles from Wurzburg, located in a rural country where the chief occupation is farming. Cows or oxen pulled the farm wagons—the German army had drafted most of the horses, which left cows to serve as workhorses.

I found only about twenty of the company still there, since most of the men had been in the company since 1942 and were on the way home. Many new men had replaced the men who went home. I wrote, "Everything is mixed up because no one knows anyone else or cares what happens." I got a job working in the supply room working under the new Supply Sergeant William Reopell, a funny little pipe smoker from New England. (I corresponded with him until his death in 1998).

My main job at least for the first week was to keep the fire in the stove going. A main interest was to listen to the World Series on the radio. The games were between the Chicago Cubs and the New York Yankees—the last time the Cubbies were in the world series.

Work finally came in; new overcoats issued and rifles turned in. To soldiers, this meant the war was finally over when their weapons were removed. We spent almost every night in the Red Cross in Achaffenberg (a large city nine miles from Sulzbach) getting coffee and doughnuts and watching movies.

---

[167] PFC Dunham was one of the men in the stockade who I was guarding in Camp Laguna.

Rumors spread that men with sixty points would soon go home, yet on October 9th, 1945 word came that men with sixty-four points or less would join the 90th Division and that their trip home would be delayed by a month or more. This almost destroyed morale but the men soon adjusted to the new reality.

In a letter dated October 15 to my sister, I wrote,

> *"Alles Kaput. Everyone's morale is lower than whale poop lately because of the news that we won't go home for a while. We can't understand the lack of shipping because we know that they have the shipping if they would only use them. I hope they work something out before long because everyone here is getting very disgusted at being shoved from one outfit to another."*

I also reported that we had been busy handing out clothing. It seems we ordered clothing for 164 men, but before the clothing came in seventy men moved out and ninety men came in. This, I might add, made for confusion in assigning clothing.

Two officers from the Inspector General's office came in and asked many questions. Sergeant Roepel turned A Company's equipment in at a depot in Munich (valued at one million dollars) and got only a Sergeant's signature on the receipt. They started to accuse Sergeant Roepel with turning equipment into the black market, which was a thriving business in Europe in the last days of the war.

I spoke up and said that even though I was in England at that time, I considered him a very honest person. I also pointed out that he took over the supply room with little or no instructions when the supply men went home on points. I also said that he was faced with much confusion at the equipment depot and dealt in good faith with the sergeants that met him. After much discussion they accepted my explanation and closed the investigation.

As they were leaving, one of them asked when should they come back. I replied "Next month at two o'clock." The answer came, "Don't get smart!" and then they left. The typical attitude of a homebound GI was, "They can't do anything to us but take away our cookies."

The men who had less than sixty-four points were transferred to the 90th Division. This was our first experience with the pleasure of boxcars (also known as "forty-or-eight's," referring to their capacity to hold either forty men or eight horses.) We rode in these small, cramped cars for fifteen hours.

From my letter of November 6, 1945:

"There were thirty in the car with all of our baggage, so it was rather crowded. I found a corner and slept pretty (well), despite the fact that I couldn't stretch out, as each man was allotted a space of 3' x 2'. They had a fire in the car on a piece of tin, which took off a lot of the chill, but it smoked so much they threw it off around 1 a.m. One of the other cars caught fire when a can of gas tipped over which they were burning. Three guys jumped out before they put it out with eight blankets. Nobody knows what happened to them, but I imagine they made it out OK."

What experiences we don't have in the army!

I also wrote in my letter about the housing in German barracks that had all the modern conveniences, such as plates to eat from and showers. There was a price to pay since division headquarters were across the parade grounds. I noted, "We can stand more training for a while I guess..."

The letter closed by speculation of departure to the U.S.: "The 90th is to sail five days after the 79th. But don't ask me when the 79th sails because I don't know."

"The U.S. occupation forces had football teams representing the First Army and the Third Army. We were advised of the big game in Nurenburg on a Friday. Thirteen of us jumped in the truck for a sixty-five mile trip in the rain. When we arrived, the truth came out: the game was on Saturday. The only choice we had was to go to the Red Cross Club to thaw out over five or six cups of coffee, doughnuts and three K Rations." I mentioned all of this in a letter of November 10th, 1945.

The next day we repeated the process, although this time we saw a very good football game with 60,000 others. I don't remember the score, but after the game we had trouble finding our truck. When we found the truck, we joined 50,000 other men peeing beside their trucks before the long rides home.

In a letter to my folks dated November 10, I described the rubble that was Nurenburg.

"The only way I know how to describe Nurenburg is to imagine a town almost as large as St. Paul, with the downtown entirely flattened, burned out, or otherwise made uninhabitable by bombs. After looking at so much wreckage over here, one gets used to it, but many times I wonder how the places looked before the war, who lived there, and where they are now. Many are still under the wreckage because the houses fell in on them before they could get out. The effectiveness of our bombing wasn't only in hitting factories, but in hitting so many dwellings, cutting water mains, etc.

"What good are factories if there isn't anyone to work in them? In the Ruhr, the factories were so well scattered that they couldn't hit them very well, so they hit everything around

them even if they didn't hit the factory. So it doesn't make much sense to preach to the German people in Hamburg, Berlin, etc. on how the Germans bombed civilians in Warsaw, Rotterdam, London, etc. "

There is now a movement in Germany that accuses the allies of killing hundreds of thousands of people in bombing raids that were nothing more than genocide. They couldn't get a hearing right after World War II because of the worldwide hatred of everything German.

My memories of the German fall weather is of gray, cold days with widowed women trudging along pulling wagons filled with wooden branches to heat their homes. People were permitted to go into the forest to clear brush to use as well. The smell of wood smoke was heavy in the air. Fifty years later, when the wife and I went walking in the twilight in Munich, the wood smoke smell brought me back to 1945. My mind could still see the same women scurrying home, trying to rush home to beat curfew that started at nightfall.

I wrote to my sister:

"It seems that the more time one has the less one does, we have been laying on our fat rear ends for the last week. (Emphasis on the fat!) It seems, I never have any ambition. One of the boys has a guitar and plays it most of the day. He used to play in a big orchestra in the states and is pretty good. He can play hillbilly, popular, classical and otherwise. It is pleasant to hear someone play a guitar that doesn't play the same old chord and the same old tune.

"The U.S. Army, one of the best fighting machines ever put together, was now comprised of individual soldiers all wanting to go home as soon as possible. The morale was not made better by the weekly reports that we would start for

*home within the next two weeks. These rumors are the little
things that shouldn't worry us. Little operators have to depend
on big time operators (BTO's) to take care of things like
moving to the boat."*

One Sunday we were awakened at 5:00 a.m. to go and
search many German homes looking for pistols, rifles and US
equipment. Four of us guarded the place while two MPs went
through everything in the place. We finished Monday
afternoon. After searching most of the town, they found a
couple pistols, and various PX items, which had been given
to the women for doing washing for the soldiers, so nothing
was done to them, but the ones that had pistols would be
prosecuted. The people were used to searches going back to
the Nazi years, but a few elderly people were frightened by
the searches.

The third Thanksgiving Day was celebrated in typical army
fashion. Breakfast at 7:30, church at 11:00, and the big meal
at 4:30. The meal consisted of one pound of turkey per man,
dressing, mashed potato, giblet gravy, asparagus, coffee, rolls,
ice cream, apple pie, and fruitcake. I wrote that it was it very
well cooked and tasted exceptionally good, and that I was
still stuffed at 10 p.m. Some of the men were still hungry as
they took a half of a turkey to eat in their rooms.

I also advised her, in this same letter, that we would leave
for Marseilles in the next week. Forty of us loaded on a boxcar
to start the long journey home. The boxcar ride wasn't so bad,
as our morale was high at the thought of going home. The
79th Division was not permitted to march through Paris in
August 1944, but now we saw Paris from the sliding door of a
boxcar as a part of the 90th Division.

After clearing Paris, we headed south through the Rhone River valley. The train stopped for a toilet break. I got out and squatted down to do my business. A DP train on an adjacent track stopped also. A woman got out of the train and squatted down not three feet from me (personal modesty was a casualty of war). After finishing I gave her some toilet paper, which she used, before each of us returned to our respective trains. I think of this event, often wondering whether she went to Russia to face a concentration camp in Siberia, or death. Stalin sent most of the returning DP to prison camps in Siberia.

The Calais staging area was located in a God-forsaken flat area swept by strong cold winds off the Mediterranean. I described it as a place near the mountains containing gravel, clay, and rocks. The room I was in housed about twenty men in bunks with tables for card games or reading. Our only duties were to a formation at 8:00 a.m., breakfast, lunch, and dinner, and free time for most of the day. The men paired off for Pinochle and other games. One of the men would shoot the moon in bidding, so no one wanted to partner with him. After much arm-twisting, I agreed to partner with him. We lost every hand due to poor bidding. This experience makes me avoid card games to this day!

The food started out tasting good but men with nothing to do stole rations from the mess hall, making for lean meals later during our stay. Company A had a cook named Herman, who would tell us in the chow line. "I'm eating good." Then men from our company began to say, "I'm eating good, Herman!"

WAITING FOR THE SHIP HOME

From a letter to my sister dated December 5, 1945:

"I quote the information put out tonight. We are sailing on the US Mariposa on December 12 and will arrive in Boston

[on] December 20. Most of the division will leave here in the next few days, but they are going by liberty ships, which take fourteen days or so to cross...I saw the Mariposa at LeHavre, so I know it is a good boat."

Note: we actually sailed for Hampton Roads, Virginia.

The 12th of December finally arrived after much anticipation. Duffel bags were packed—although on this trip we didn't have to carry rifles, ammunition, belts, and canteens! I might add that morale was sky-high, with everyone eagerly anticipating going home. Looking around at the fifteen men seated with me on the truck, I couldn't help but notice that many men that came over with us would not be going home with us, but were either buried in Normandy or Lorraine, or severely wounded and going home another way.

ON THE SHIP

The day was a sunny, cold day and the Mediterranean Sea was sparkling in the distance. We passed through the warehouse district and then the wharfs, where the huge, two-stacker ship the Mariposa was docked. The Mariposa was a large ship of the Mattson lines that sailed from Los Angeles and San Francisco to Hawaii and on to Tokyo.

After walking up the gangplank, twelve of us were assigned to a deluxe, above- deck cabin, complete with a fancy bathtub and fixtures.

Within fifteen minutes, some officers appeared who had been sent to compartments below deck. As you might imagine, they wanted to kick us out of our fancy quarters. They made their case to the assigning officer, who advised them that the officers had had it good during the war, and that now that the war was over these combat soldiers would get the good accommodations. The complaining officers returned to their quarters with their tails between their legs.

The ship pulled out of the dock after dark; while we could not see the sights of this scenic area, we enjoyed watching the thousands of lights.

USS Mariposa

THE ARMY'S PAY POLICY

Before we boarded the ship we were paid in American dollars. But we could take only three months pay on the ship. This restriction was due to the black market activities of some of the men. One man, a complete sad sack, had thousands of dollars to get home legally or otherwise. He asked some men to take one hundred dollars with the understanding they could keep twenty dollars. He tried to collect his money and was often told, "I don't know what you're talking about, Kupersmith!" How much he collected I will never know. The Mariposa had long corridors that were filled every day with crapshooters and poker players. This continued for the entire voyage.

I spent most of the time on deck, enjoying the almost warm South Atlantic air. The morale of the men was the reverse of the voyage we took in April 1944. Now the men were going home having survived the war. There still was a steady stream of men that stopped by just to talk. In mid-voyage a storm hit that was not too difficult on a large ship. One day, I came on deck when the ship rolled down with a violent motion sent me headlong across the deck until I came to a stop against the railing.

HOME AT LAST

The days passed quickly, and on the tenth day we pulled into Hampton Roads, Virginia. When the ship docked, we had no welcoming group; no Red Cross girls with coffee and doughnuts. Our welcoming committee was comprised of four little black kids waving at us from the shore. I am still a little upset when I see bands and celebrations for troops who served for less than six months in Iraq.

Rudy Thell gave me his ticket for a welcome home dinner at Camp Patrick Henry. I don't remember anything about the dinner, but I must have gone. This softens my view of lack of welcome home.

Camp Patrick Henry was our home for three or four days. Finally we boarded a large steam train of the Norfolk and Western, heading north and west. When the train stopped in Roanoke, Virginia, I remember the coal cars on the track and the people scurrying to get out of the cold December air.

I only remember going through Charleston, West Virginia and Chicago before pulling into Camp McCoy, Wisconsin to stay in barracks, which seemed so familiar after thirty months at war.

During the exit interview, I was asked if I would take army experiences with me into civilian life. I replied there wasn't much demand for a minesweeper and machine gun man in civilian life. We were permitted to keep our clothing, overcoats, etc. I turned in my pack and some other items.

The discharge papers were ready on the morning of December 30, 1945. I was given $6.30 bus fare from Sparta, WI to Lyle, MN. I took a bus from Sparta to LaCrosse, then caught a train to Minneapolis. The train was crowded, so I had to stand or more correctly sit on my duffel bag. Despite all this, it seemed good to mix with the general population again.

When I arrived in Minneapolis, my uncle, my sister, and my cousin Margerie met me. This was a very special time for my aunt and uncle, since they had adopted a son Carl, Jr. about six months old. I stayed with them for several days, then took a train from Minneapolis to Los Angeles, making connections in Omaha. The Challenger train was crowded, but I got a seat and enjoyed the country from the train window. The new morality of a post-war world was on display on a seat close by, as a sailor and a young woman had sex under a blanket in the darkened coach.

My Aunt Allie and Uncle Clifford met me at the station. They drove me to San Diego the next day. We had a good homecoming and I enjoyed the month of January in their new home. The month passed quickly and it was time to leave again for the second semester at St. Olaf College. My Aunt Inez and her prospective husband picked me up in San Diego and drove me to Los Angeles where I spent the night and caught the train for Minneapolis. I got off the train from Minneapolis to Northfield on a cold February day after a snowfall of eight to ten inches the day before. On the taxi ride to the campus the radio played "A Winter Wonderland," which since then has always reminded me of the snowy wonderland views in the taxi.

I am now back at Yitterbo Hall, the same old dormitory where my father stayed from 1912-1916. The dorm had been remodeled with bathrooms on each floor. I had a new roommate, Harold Hagen, but many of the men that left here with me in 1943 returned OK—Bruce Govig, Bob Fingarson, and Ralph Rusley in particular.

The adventure that had taken me over 10,000 miles and provided many life-changing experiences was now over. Thirty months before, I left an immature nineteen year old and had returned a mature twenty-two year old ready for a career as a student and later a government official.

U.S.A.T. MARIPOSA

(Built in 1931 by the Bethlehem Steel Corporation, Quincy, Massachusetts. Operated during world War I, by Matson Navigation Company and JESA.)

Measuring 601 feet in length, 79 feet in beam, and with a 28-foot draft, this ship had a gross tonnage of 18,100. She had a steam-turbine drive, twin propellers, and was rated at 20 knots. Her Passenger capacity was 1, 243. In contrast, during wartime, she had accommodations for 4, 272 Officers and enlisted troops. Her service was termed worldwide, for her duties carried her to all the oceanic theaters of war during that conflict.

Her first trip was from San Francisco to Melbourne and Brisbane, Australia with troops. She departed January 12 and returned back to San Francisco on 8 May 1942. She departed for Charleston, South Carolina where she took on troops and departed for Bombay and Karachi, India and departed on 28 May. She returned back to New York, then departed on 20 October 1942 to England and North Africa, returning to New York on 8 December 1942. She departed for South America then continued on to the Suez Canal to Bombay and Cape Town, South Africa. Returning back to New York 16 April 1943. She departed for Casablanca up to 10 July 1943). She made three trips to Casablanca.

On 9 September 1943 she departed New York for South America and continued on to Australia. She departed Sydney for San Francisco, California and remained there until 6 December 1943 when she departed Massachusetts and made runs to England from Boston until September 1944.

On 1 December 1944 she departed Boston with troops and landed in Southern France. The rest of her time in service was spent making runs between Boston and Le Harve. Her last run was from Hampton Roads to Marseilles, departing 29 November 1945.

The Mariposa experienced one of the most interesting and busy careers of all the troopships of World War II. Following the war, Mariposa was placed in the Reserve Fleet. In 1953, she was "sold foreign," going over to the Home Lines, which reconverted her to a peacetime passenger ship. Renamed **Homeric,** she entered service on the Southampton Le Havre-Quebec run, mainly carrying emigrants. Occasionally, she took American tourists on a cruise out of New York to the West Indies. Later she was laid up; and in January 1974, she arrived at Kaohsiung. Taiwan and commenced being broken up for her scrap metal value.

18

Life in the Army

HUMOR AND RUMORS

Often the men could do little to affect their situation. Their only recourse was to laugh at their own dilemma. It was this humor that Bill Mauldin tried to capture in his cartoons of GIs, "Who are able to fight in a ruthless war against ruthless enemies, and still grin at themselves."

The army in combat lived on rumors. Ernie Pyle stated rumor mongering was a very useful diversion for the GI. "When the Army doesn't have women, ice cream, beer or clean clothes, it certainly has to have something to look forward to, even if only a faint hope for some kind of change that lies buried in an illogical rumor."[168]

COMPANY CHARACTERS

A company had its share of men who were unusual and separated from the crowd.

A certain PFC would open a beer bottle with his teeth until he cracked one or more teeth.

Another PFC advised his mates that he would drink a bottle of catsup for five dollars. He did this only once, as he found catsup to be a strong disgusting mess to drink. He also found his stomach was upset for two or more days after this incident.

---

[168] Pyle, Brave Men 90

Four men would go to the beer PX at 7:00 p.m. Each man would take an empty wooden case and set it beside himself before the serious beer drinking would start. The next three hours would see one bottle after another consumed until his empty case was filled with 24 bottles and it was ten o'clock, time to go home.

Rudy Thell reported that a soldier in the second platoon spied a dead German on the ground. This soldier stopped, bent down and cut the German's finger off just to get the man's ring.

"FOR THE GOOD TIMES" *

From the war movies, one would get the impression that action was continuous, with the artillery shelling and bombing all the time.

The reality was many periods completely free from action. Our squad used these times for talking, telling stories, or just horsing around.

These men were from many places and backgrounds— Pennsylvania, Alabama, Louisiana, Virginia, Illinois, Indiana, Missouri, and elsewhere. This was new to me, coming from a Scandinavian background in Minnesota. The average soldier was not an enthusiastic warrior; yet to his surprise he discovered the soldiering life was not completely negative. He usually would fondly remember comrades who saved his life; shared every experience during good times or bad. In fact, the enduring emotion of war is comradeship which more than made up for the hardships and the only redeeming factors the bravery and their devotion to one another.[169]

---

* From a song of the time by that name.
[169] Kindsvatter 179, 180

COMPANY MUSICIANS

Company A had country and bluegrass musicians. One played the guitar and one played the fiddle. They played and sang well into the night on weekends and holidays. The songs they played included *"There's a Ramshackle Shack down in Old Caroline," "Columbus Stockade Blues," "Going Down that Road Feeling Bad," "Take Me Back and Try one more time," "Wabash Cannonball,"* etc. I learned to love country music from listening to them play. We also listened to Hispanic music. When a Mexican soldier came in as a replacement, he and Chico would sing Mexican and other Hispanic songs well into the night.

RECYCLING

The Army recycled metals and fats. Part of a KP's job was to take the ends out of cans and then flatten the cans. We also saved grease and lard.

UNIT COHESION—HISTORY

The U.S. infantry divisions, most of them mobilized in 1941-2, trained where unit cohesion was given great importance. For example, the 79th Division organized in June 1942 went through maneuvers in Tennessee and the Arizona desert. The two years of training and working together made the division a well-trained fighting unit.

The 7th Army had a replacement system that did not permit the fighting units to "dwindle down to the nub." Even in the rifle battalions that suffered the most casualties in the campaign in the high Vosges, the total strength was not permitted to drop below 679. Thus replacements joined units that although bloodied still retained family or team identities developed in pre-campaign training. This provided a degree of comfort and the feeling of belonging essential for the maintenance of high morale. [170]

Lieutenant General Patch and his commander of the Seventh Army were able to commit well-trained, cohesive and often battle units in a terrain that made any operations a nightmare. They maintained the effectiveness of these units by well-timed replacement of these units, the units involved- the 45th, 3rd, 36th, and 79th Divisions were given one or two weeks rest.[171]

The most important thing that holds soldiers together was unit cohesion. The development of feeling of family in the platoons and squads are qualities most World War II veterans point to when they say how they survived and won.[172] The stress of war shows the importance of unit cohesion. As one soldier wrote, "One's values change when faced with the rigors of combat. The everyday living and sharing of hardships and danger with buddies result in a closeness and trust that would be difficult to duplicate anywhere else." [173]

Cohesion sustained the units' effectiveness and morale. The breakdown of cohesion with casualties intensified the uncertainties and fears facing soldiers further diminished the fighting power of the unit.[174] That the Wehrmacht kept its cohesion through the course of catastrophes was due to superior training of the junior officers. These officers were grounded in every detail and doctrine, but they were also encouraged to think and act for themselves in a battle. They were also critical to the primary bonding that was so strong and traditional at the squad level.

---

[170] Bonn 119
[171] Bonn 137
[172] Ambose, Citizen Soldiers 14
[173] Willis 24
[174] Carafano 40-41

What are the reasons that combat men kept going day after day through the times of heavy casualties? Discipline, training and unit cohesion were the large items. But for many soldiers it was a sense of having no option but to annihilate the German army. They also realized the only way for them to go home was to keep going forward.[175]

BATTLE FATIGUE

There are limits to human endurance. World War II showed us the limits of human endurance, which often resulted in battle fatigue.

One of the first signs of battle fatigue is a soldier reciting the names of the men killed or wounded. After this then the solider will say, "I will be next to be killed." Then he would break down and start sobbing and crying.

In *"America's Forgotten Army,"* Charles Whiting describes the history of battle fatigue in Europe from North Africa to France:

"In North Africa at the disastrous rout of the Kasserine Pass in February 1943, up to 34% of all casualties were mental, worse still only 3% of the GIs who broke down with shell shock, as it was called, ever returned to action.

"In Italy in a period of forty-four days, the First Armored Division, mental casualties accounted for a staggering 54% of all losses. The situation in Northern Europe was no different.

"By January 1945, almost 100,000 men had been diagnosed with "combat fatigue" in the bitter fighting in the Huertgen Forest—"The Death Factory," as GIs called it. Companies and even battalions had fled. Division

---

[175] Ambose, Citizen Soldiers 393, 394

commanders set up their psychiatric centers or "rest centers" as they were officially called to handle the flood of soldiers who had broken down. The men would be given drugs and permitted to sleep for three days before being sent back to the front. The reasoning was that once the men got as far back as a general hospital they would never be returned to the duty. However, many of these men who returned to duty usually broke down again."[176]

After the completion of thirteen weeks' college in England, I spent several days in Camp Lucky Strike, an infamous "repple depple" waiting for transportation to Germany. I talked to a soldier who said he was in a camp for battle fatigue. One day noise of shells coming in and planes strafing, etc., made many of the battle-fatigued men crawl under cots to get away from shelling noises. The man said he lay in his cot laughing at the men crawling on the floor. Doctors came and told him he had no symptoms of battle fatigue and would be sent back to his unit.

The army directed the divisions to appoint psychiatric officers who went through a month-long course on medical psychiatry.

Even though this training was limited, army units developed fairly effective procedures for these stress patients. Most cases were treated at the battalion level. For exhaustion, the battalion surgeon would hold the man at the aid station for up to twenty-four hours, often under sedation. Sleep, hot food, a change in uniform and informal group therapy often proved sufficient to return the man to duty where he could function in combat. Only the most severely disturbed cases were evacuated.[177]

---

[175] Whiting 136, 137
[177] Carafano 58

THE BREAKING POINT

A chaplain was usually at the aid station to provide spiritual support, though more often he assisted the doctor and the medics. The lightly wounded were patched up and returned to duty and the seriously injured were stabilized to the rear.

The final stop for the wounded was the regimental casualty collection point, where he was evacuated to an Army hospital or evacuation hospital.*

Although hospital staffs were far from the front, they were not exempt from long hours and overwhelming responsibility. Staff worked in two twelve-hour shifts. Each hospital used four operating tables for major surgery, two for fractures, and three for minor surgery. During major battles the tables were in use eighteen to twenty-four hours a day.[178]

CHAPLAINS OR FIGHTING PARSONS

Among the men who wore the Cross of Lorraine there was a small group, numbering never more than fifteen, whose influence was far out of proportion to their rank or numbers. This group was the chaplains, whose presence represented their faith both in God and to the men in trying circumstances.[179]

They lived with the men, they shared all the dangers of the battle at the front, caring for the wounded and comforting the men who suffered. Statistics reveal their record: eleven Purple Hearts, eight Silver Stars and two Bronze Stars; two killed in action and seven evacuated due to wounds. By V.E. day only

---

* Divisions usually used the division band on the offensive as litter bearers for COBRA. First Army expected 600 casualties per division per day. To handle these casualties, VII Corps was to have five hospitals supporting the offensive.

---

[178] Max S. Allen Medicine Under Canvas 111
[179] Province 300, 318

seven were left. During the ten months of combat twenty-four chaplains served and fourteen had been lost through combat or non-combat reasons.

Three chaplains served with each regiment, two with division artillery, two with medicine clearing company, one with special troops, and one in rear-echelon. The bulk of their time was spent at forward medical stations where they tended to the needs of the wounded. They also accompanied the litter bearers forward to evacuate the seriously wounded.

"The chaplain section was, of course, charged with the spiritual guidance of the Third Army troops, but additionally the chaplains were expected to have a good effect on the morale within the Third Army." In a paper that General Patton wrote in 1919, he indicated that the mission of the chaplains was to "fight the devil." In parentheses, he added, "usually unsuccessfully." An average of 320 chaplains served within the Third Army, representating 25 different denominations.[180]

ARMY MEDICAL UNITS

The cornerstone of U.S. military medical system was the medical battalion, which provided detachments to each regiment. The detachment provided enlisted medics to the forward units. The life of each medic was dangerous and difficult. For example, in the two weeks prior to COBRA, the 9th Division had twenty-one medical personnel killed, 159 wounded and fifty-nine captured.

Despite losses, medics still operated with the forward units. The reason they stayed forward was that statistically, seven out every ten wounds that had to be treated resulted from

---

[180] History of the 79th 156

combat were not fatal if treated on the spot. This treatment usually involved stopping the bleeding, treating for shock, and evacuating the wounded.

The first step was controlling the bleeding by applying a pressure bandage, which every soldier carried as part of his basic kit. Many medics would throw away their gas masks and fill the bag with extra bandages and other supplies.

The litter bearers carried the casualties to the battalion aid station where surgeons attended the wounded.[181]

"The medical apparatus behind the US Army in Normandy was very impressive. Before the breakthrough, First Army medical units treated 95,639 patients, the equivalent of almost six infantry divisions. Of these, 22,639 were returned to duty."[182] (For more information, see "Combat Medics" insert from 79th Division History.)

FOOD RATIONS
Army Distribution Policy

Rations were distributed on a daily basis. Each man would receive his ration every day; i.e. 3 K rations or 6 C rations. All in all, we spent only two or three days with no rations.

Tobacco and Alcohol

The tobacco companies provided massive quantities of cigarettes for the troops. This proved to be a good policy for tobacco companies, as literally millions of GIs became addicted to cigarettes. Every two weeks or so packs of cigarettes were distributed to the men. Gum and candy bars were also available. A few of my platoon-mates suggested that I should smoke to

---

[181] Carafano 56, 57
[182] Carafano 59

steady my nerves, to which I replied that I would put my nerves up against any member of the platoon. I usually traded my cigarettes for gum or candy bars.

Other tobacco such as cigars and chewing tobacco and snuff were available only occasionally. One man, desperate for chewing tobacco, shredded cigarettes and put the tobacco in his mouth, with less than satisfactory results.

CLASSES OF RATIONS

Class A-Fresh vegetables, meat, poultry, fruit, served in garrison duty.

Class B-Canned meat, vegetables, and fruit, served in field or in France.

Class C-Rations originally conceived as "A balanced meal in a can," C rations were composed of six 12-ounce cans, three of which were meat units and bread units. It also included sugar, soluble instant coffee and hard candy. The days rations provided 3,000 calories.

Despite efforts to introduce a greater variety, meat and beans, meat and vegetable hash, and vegetable stew constituted the major C ration components throughout World War II.

The GIs in Italy discovered the C rations to be almost inedible after a week or so. They were difficult to eat cold and it was very bulky to carry the six cans that made up the daily ration. My experience agrees with those troops. I found the corned beef hash was edible only if burned by the fire. I recently read the book *Is Paris Burning?*, which noted that troops of the French Second Armored Division were eating C rations on the road to Paris. This was also my experience. I thought it odd that they were eating C rations when everybody in France ate K rations, but my question was answered by reading *Breakout and Pursuit*.[183]

The arrival of the French Second Armored Division in Great Britain caused feeding problems to allies. The division included Muslims, whose religion forbade them to eat pork or drink wine. Providing rations for soldiers in Normandy was simple since each meal of K rations contained pork and the C rations contained only meat and vegetables and were without pork. The C rations were issued with the understanding that meat and beans and vegetable hash would go to the Frenchmen and the meat and vegetable stew would go to the Muslim troops.

D Rations

D rations consisted of three four-ounce chocolate bars, flavored and fortified with sucrose, skim milk, cacao fat and oatmeal flour, containing 1,800 calories each. The D ration could be issued only in extreme emergencies. They were issued to us in Normandy the first few days after our arrival.

K Rations

In 1940, Dr. Key, a nutritionist at the University of Minnesota, received a request from the War Department explaining that war had recently broken out in Europe and it was feared the U.S. would soon be involved. Dr. Key was asked to devise a nutritious ration for the paratroopers.

Dr. Key stated, "I went down to a local grocery store and picked up some food that I thought nutritious and took them back to the lab."

The first K rations were tested at Fort Snelling and more extensive tests were done several months later at Fort Benning, Georgia. The Army was impressed enough that the

―――――――――――――
[183] Blumenson 428

ration became the standard field issue to troops for the duration of the conflict.[184]

The need for a ration that had greater food value than the "D" ration and was more compact than the "C" resulted in the development of the K ration. This ration was packaged in three rectangular boxes, each small enough to fit in the pocket of a paratrooper's uniform. Each box held a separate meal, including crackers, dextrose tablets, a can of meat and egg or processed meat plus a stick of chewing gum. Another box held a fruit bar, soluble concentrated bouillon, a 2-oz bar D-ration, lemon juice powder, sugar tablets and a small roll of toilet paper. Because of its small dimensions and protective wax cardboard wrapping, it has been called, "A triumph of the packager's art."

The concentrated coffee and lemonade was the first of its kind we had seen or used. The breakfast box contained a fruit bar of figs and raisins to keep us regular. The noon ration contained a can of cheese to reduce the probability of loose bowels. The K ration could be eaten day after day without getting tiresome.

The German soldiers view of American K rations as presented in Wolf T. Zoepp's Seven Days in January:

"The American 70th Infantry ran when attacked leaving everything behind in their flight. Most of the American foxholes were empty, their occupants having left to avoid capture. Knowing by heart what to expect in a Red Army foxhole, our men were curious about what American foxholes contained, as they were the first ones they had encountered. They searched them thoroughly. They found unbelievable riches, including lots of cigarettes! But what was the lengthy brown box covered with wax papers? On first sight it looked

---

[184] Minnesota Magazine, March-April 2001 30

like a pack of dynamite, but then somebody took heart and bravely explored further. He was rewarded for his courage—to his great enjoyment it contained food of the highest quality! It was an American "K-ration." Only the cursing of their commanding officer could make the men cease stuffing their jackets full of this bounty, abandon further searching and move on in the fight."[185]

5 in 1 Rations

A need for a more complete ration for small, isolated units such as tank crews, combat engineers, etc. led the quartermasters to design a ration to feed five men for one day- thus the name "5 in 1". This ration permitted the preparation of warm meals by men with limited cooking experience or cooking facilities.

A breakfast would consist of dehydrated tomato juice, whole-wheat cereal, soluble coffee, sugar and canned milk, and the best canned bacon I ever ate. With the cereal, all you had to do was open the box and add water to the dry milk found on the cereal. We would have a K-ration for lunch, and dinner would include meat and vegetable stew, vanilla pudding powder or canned glorified rice whipped cream, and pineapple, a supply of biscuits, and a fruit spread. The nutrition value of all this food was a whopping 3,668 calories.

A Neat Can Opener

A small can opener was issued with the 5 in 1 rations. It measured $1\frac{1}{2}$ inches by $\frac{1}{16}$th, a blade opened each can with minimum effort. I still have one placed under glass with the rest of my Army decorations.

---

[185] Zoepf 118

Army Cake

The cooks would make extra batter when cooking pancakes for breakfast. They would add sugar, vanilla, etc. and put it in the oven to produce a cake. For frosting they added layers of orange marmalade and peanut butter. The resulting cake was acceptable for men in the field and provided a dessert for an otherwise drab diet.

SPAM

Spam, the best of the luncheon meats, is made by the Hormel Company of Austin, Minnesota. The soldiers called the luncheon meat served in the army spam even though the military never served the real thing. The minds of millions of GIs were poisoned against eating Hormel's product because of their dislike for the army's luncheon. These days, spam also refers to unwanted e-mail messages. In fact, an anti-spam act is awaiting passage in Congress.

PERSONAL HYGIENE

Five gallons of treated water was issued per squad per day. From this five gallons we had to fill drinking water in canteens as well as use water for washing and shaving. The helmet was ideal for washing ourselves, after the helmet liner was removed. We shaved our beards once a week or so. The lieutenant would order every man to shave and it was a great experience to shave in cold water. We went from June 1944 to May 1945 without sleeping in a regular bed. The damage to kidneys meant any camping nights were painful sleeping on the ground.

BAD WEATHER

Bad weather played a large part in weakening those who had prolonged duty in the front lines. The incessant Normandy rain, followed by blistering summer heat made life miserable for all. As one soldier wrote, "If I don't get a chance to bathe and a change of clothes pretty soon I'm going to have to burn the ones I'm wearing. I don't think the stink will ever come out of them. All I've had is a wash out of my helmet, what we call a whore's bath.[186]

As the summer passed, the First Army increased the laundry, repair and bath units in Normandy. It assigned to the VII Corps four laundry companies and a bath section. They erected twenty-four hot showers that ran 15 hours a day.[187]

By July 1944 soldiers also received a change of clothes- mostly underwear.[188]

WARM CLOTHING

Movies such as *Saving Private Ryan, The Longest Day,* and other pictures from or about World War II showed GIs in jackets in June, 1944. In real life, GIs wore warm clothing because the climate is similar to northern Minnesota or even Yellowstone. The temperature seldom topped 70 degrees and with the cold wind blowing off the channel it was downright cold even in the summer months.

The summer uniform consisted of:

- Underwear
- Wool trousers, olive drab
- Fatigue trousers
- Wool olive-drab shirt
- Fatigue shirt
- Field jacket

---

[186] Giles, GI Journal 50
[187] Carafano 53
[188] Carafano 53

We slept in our clothes from June 1, 1944 to May 8, 1945. In Normandy, we slept in a foxhole, sometimes without any blankets. We changed our underwear every three months if we were lucky. A common joke made the rounds: an NCO would announce, "We are going to change our underwear. Joe, change with Pete. Pete, change with John, etc."

In June 1944, several days the temperature reached 70 degrees plus, which caused some discomfort, but we took off our jackets and extra shirts. On sunny warm days we sat in the sun to absorb the rays.

The winter uniform

- Heavy underwear—comparable to thermal
- Olive-drab wool trousers
- Wool shirt
- Fatigue trousers and shirt
- A sweater or field jacket
- New winter jacket
- Leather boots with rubber bottoms

Wet cold conditions are highly conducive to the following disabling injuries: immersion foot which results from contact with water...under 50 degrees for twelve hours or more; trench foot, which results from the same conditions for forty-eight to seventy-two hours, and frost bite which is crystallization of tissue and fluids in the skin resulting from temperatures of 32 degrees or less for periods that vary with wind velocity and humidity. Diseases such as pneumonia are also a constant threat in cold weather. During the second half of October in the Vosges, it rained every day but one.[189] November brought much more rain and in the higher elevations, the first snows. December and January were snowy and frigid.[190]

---

[189] Journals of U.S. 3rd, 36th, 45th and 79th Divisions
[190] Bonn 27

Colonel Sterling Wood, Commander of the 313th Infantry witnessed many trench foot cases in military hospitals as a patient. On his return to duty he ordered all of us to keep extra socks dry by pinning socks inside our fatigue shirts. We also placed boots under us as a pillow to prevent them from freezing.

Showers were very rare, in fact we went for six weeks without a shower. Since we were in the fresh air, no one noticed any body odors. The army would place a tent shower by a river and pump the water through a heater to the shower. Men would be run through thirty at a time, allotting time to soap up, rinse off and out. They often issued underwear and socks. One shower in November I got all soaped up, only to have the water go ice cold and leave me with the problem of having to rinse off in cold water when it was 35 to 40 degrees outside.

Slit trenches (latrines) were dug in every place we bivouacked. They were covered with dirt before we moved on. A cross was typically put up to mark an old latrine, with a sign that would read, "Old latrine 6-20-44". There was once a funny cartoon by Bill Mauldon that showed a Frenchman placing flowers on an old latrine cross. The French water caused loose bowels, which was a large problem. The men who drank hard cider also had problems with their bowels.

THE 79TH DIVISION AIR CORPS

The American artillery was considered the best in World War II. The 79th Division Air Corps was responsible for making the artillery fire devastating for the Germans.

Piper Cubs known as L-4s were unarmed and had little defense against enemy attack. They relied on slow speed of seventy-five miles per hour and very low altitude to protect them from high-flying fighter planes, and their great maneuverability to evade flak from the ground. Two Piper Cubs were attached to each artillery battalion and to the division artillery. The men flying the planes were artillerymen and not pilots who were experts in figuring range, etc.

The planes went into action D-plus-8 and had their first casualty on that day. Lt. Lock G. Chan disappeared and was never heard from again. In Normandy, pilots flew without spotters, which lessened their effectiveness.

From June 19th, when they hopped the hedgerows, to V.E. day in the rubble of the Ruhr, the Cubs flew 3,000 combat hours in 2,241 missions for a total of almost 380,000 miles. Many of these missions were flown in bad weather, which grounded the P-47s and the Luftwaffe held special missions to shoot down the Cubs.

The pilots and spotters suffered eight casualties; four downed by German aircraft; two by ack-ack, one in a crash landing, and one was MIA.

The troops on the ground enjoyed watching the small planes because we knew that the Germans would be in for a pasting from our artillery. The most fun was seeing them dive to get away from planes or ack-ack.

The Cubs proved their worth in fighting in the Seine beachhead. Targets for the division and corps artillery fire caused damage to the Germans and broke up their counter attack.

It was this type of performance by the observation planes that enabled the 201 FA Battalion to earn the Presidential Citation during the Nordwind Offensive in Alsace. The accurate fire due to observation by the small planes amazed the German soldiers who, later in the POW enclosures expressed wonder and surprise at the horror of the U.S. artillery, It must be "automatic" they said, because no one could send that many shells manually. This was a compliment to the pilots, the POW's said. You must have inside information, since no one could spot targets that well.[191] [192]

79th MILITARY GOVERNMENT

The 79th Military Government (MG) unit entered a town usually with the forward troops. After contacting the FFI (Free French of the Interior) and local leaders, a mayor was appointed and steps were taken to establish civil government.

In the rat-race days after the breakthrough, many of the MG units were scattered in towns miles apart. In Normandy, civil affairs faced a serious health problem with thousands of dead animals to be buried by civilians to prevent disease.

In Alsace-Lorraine with its many Germans who were Nazi sympathizers, the MG unit had to investigate choices for civil government before civil government could be established again. At Hagenau, when a withdrawal had to be made from divisions' positions along the Maginot Line, the French government had trains running from Alsatian towns to Hagenau and it was up to civil affairs to round up people. 12,500 people were evacuated before the German army occupied the towns.

The problems were compounded when the division drove into the Ruhr where 75% of cities like Essen and Dortmund were destroyed. There was no water or electricity and very little food. Hundreds of thousands of displaced people mostly from Poland and the Soviet Union further complicated the situation. To feed, house, and guard was the first problem, following the

---

[191] Lorraine Cross—Weekly Paper of 79th Vol 1 No. 10 p. 155 July 10, 1945
[192] 79th Division History 155

need to setting up an administration run by Germans. Order was established with help from reconnaissance troops and the military police. Camps were set up for different nationalities (see earlier chapter on Displaced Person Camps).

When the 79th Division was stationed in the Sudetenland, their main job was to feed and care for the German civilians and help Czech officials reinstate civilian government. [193]

COMMUNICATIONS—79TH SIGNAL COMPANY

The 79th Signal Company laid 3,775 miles of wire, and its message center jeeps covered 144,000 miles or 5 times around the world.

During the drive to the battles in Normandy, the primary means of communications was field wire. Heavy artillery shelling kept the repairmen on the run twenty-four hours a day. After the breakthrough and the drive across France, the units traveled too fast for wire, so radio communication predominated. During the German Nordwind Offensive in Alsace in January 1945, the 79th Division was strung out over an area previously covered by three divisions. The divisions withdrew to the Maginot line and were reinforced by two armored and two infantry divisions. None of these new divisions had signal companies with them so the main signal load fell on the 79th Signal Company. (See "Unit Cohesion" for further information on the 42nd, 63rd and 10th divisions.)[194]

---

[193] Lorraine Cross Vol 1, No 3 June 26, 1945
[194] 79th Division History 152

463ᴿᴰ ANTI-AIRCRAFT BATTALION

The 463ʳᵈ Automatic Weapons Battalion joined the 79ᵗʰ Division on June 29, 1944 and remained with the unit until May 1945. Each of the battalions' four batteries was composed of two platoons of two sections each. Each section has a 40mm Bofors and an M-51 (A British 4.5mm machine gun). The M-51's specialty is low flying planes, while the Bofors can reach medium altitudes.[195]

INFORMAL ORGANIZATION

After a few days in combat the formal organization broke down. Sergeant Motter couldn't adapt to realities of combat and broke down after a few days. Corporal Sheets was all shook up but was wounded before he developed battle fatigue. The informal organization took over and three men ran the squad: Technical Sergeant James Johnson, C. Willis Nale (a replacement), and me.

We got the assignments and organized each job. In combat, the men who can do the job were the ones selected. In early July, I started private meetings with Lieutenant Joseph Macrino. We met weekly to talk over the situation and what the men were concerned about. The lieutenant needed someone to discuss things with, and since I was one of two men that had any college training, we hit it off immediately. These liaisons lasted until May 8, 1945. In fact, a replacement soldier was in our squad for one week before he realized I was only a PFC.

In the fall we received two replacements from the infantry division that went to Iceland in 1942. Each one showed the

---

[195] Lorraine Cross Vol 1, No 4 June 26, 1945

effects of long garrison duty. Sergeant Adams knew the combat engineer trade. The other soldier was a drunk. In Alsace, the working part of the squad stayed with a three-generation family. The grandparents spoke German, since Alsace was part of Germany until 1919. The younger couple spoke French since Alsace was French territory from 1919-1940. The grandchildren spoke German. The goof-off part of the squad stayed with an old lady who was senile. This group, including Sergeant Adams, raised cain from morning to evening. They killed her chickens to roast or cook and then decided if they wanted eggs, they shouldn't kill all of the chickens.

LEADERSHIP

General James H. Doolittle's definition of leadership.

Question: what would you say are the qualities of a great leader?

"... I would say the following are critical and non-negotiable: integrity, morality, understanding and accepting responsibility for your actions and providing encouragement and praise when necessary. Let the men know they can trust you, and that you have their best interest at heart, and they will follow you anywhere. Live by the same rules you enforce, and never waiver from a sound, well thought-out decision, even in the face of stiff criticism. These are the traits that define a great leader, as well as a great man. I made mistakes; I was not perfect. However, I never placed blame upon anyone else for anything that occurred under my command, that is the first trait of a bad leader. Plus, to be a good leader, you will have to follow orders as well, and not just the ones

you like. Men will follow you if they have faith in you, no doubt. But they will fight and even die if they respect you and you have their loyalty. That is earned, not given."

Excerpted from an interview conducted by Colin D. Heated on Sept 27, 1993. World War II Magazine, May 2003

AUTOMATED RECORDS SYSTEM (PUNCH CARDS)

The average strength of Patton's Third Army during combat was around 250,000 men. How was it possible that a small number of adjunct general personnel coud keep records about that many men? The answer was the Machine Records Divisions Unit, which used punched card equipment, to perform personnel accounting. The process was finished on unit record machines, also called electrical accounting machines.[196]

GERMAN MILITARY ORGANIZATION

In the mid-thirties, the Germans divided the division into panzer and infantry units. The panzer divisions were completely mechanized—tanks, self-propelled artillery, trucks, etc. Some 600,000 vehicles mobilized for the invasion of Russia.[196] The infantry divisions were organized on the World War I models. They had only a few vehicles and were reliant on horses. Gen. Halder estimated that each division needed 4,500 horses and 200 horse drawn vehicles. The German army started the war in 1939 with almost 600,000 horses.[197]

---

[196] Overy 215
[197] May 208

FIREPOWER

The MP-40 submachine gun (GIs called it the "burp gun" due to the distinctive sound it made when it fired) with which all officers and NCOs were equipped, sprayed 9mm pistol ammunition at a high rate of fire (1,200 rounds per minute) and was very effective under 100 meters range. Several of the NCOs carried Finnish-made weapons, which were even more effective due to their large-capacity, drum-type magazines.

...the German firepower...stemmed mainly from the overwhelming proportion of machine guns, while each U.S. rifle company had two .30 caliber air-cooled machine gun and nine browning automatic rifles (BAR) firing from twenty-round magainzes. Each German Jager company had twelve belt-fed MC-42 machine guns ("Hitler Saws"). The fire from the fifteen to twenty submachine guns that must have been present in each Jager Company accounted for the German firepower advantage as long as ammunition lasted.[198]

German tacticians believed the MC-42 should play a vital role in combat serving as a firebase for defense. The machine gunners loosened their traverse adjustments, pre-sighted and were able to set up their guns to make a section of the battlefield as large as 500 meters downrange virtually impossible to the infantry. If the Germans had a large number of MC-42s and were reinforced by artillery and mortar support, allied forward progress would become prohibitively expensive for allied advances. [199]

---

[198] Zoepf 146
[199] WWII Magazine, James L. Thomson, 8

Comparison of Germans and Americans as Fighters

From an interview with Fritz Schweigler:

"Schweigler,...The Americans were good, but not as good as the Germans..., they didn't have to be, that's the point. They had all the materiel. A German platoon leader had to be ready to attack with or without artillery, with or without air support. But the Americans had lots of artillery and tanks. They could just sit back and shoot and shoot and shoot. American commanders were not as aggressive. They wouldn't accept the losses a German routinely did. They didn't take as many chances. They probably figured-why should they risk heavy losses when time was on their side? Our views about the American soldiers were influenced by our fathers' experiences in the first world war: good guys, generous and they will treat you properly if you are captured. Not so with the Russians. You knew you had to fight to the last round." [200]

---

[200] David T. Zabecki — Odyssey of a Landser WWII Magazine Sept 2003 p.56

COMBAT MEDICS

Adding to the achievements Of the 79th Infantry Division during World War II is another glowing chapter—that of a small but heroic unit—the 304th Medical Battalion.

Essentially designed to save lives and conserve military strength, the 304th Medics, consisting of a well-knitted group of professional doctors and enlisted men trained to do their job under the strains of battle, received its initial training with the division in the United States.

After months of constant and intensive training under all battle conditions at Camp Blanding, Florida, and various maneuver areas, additional training for forth-coming operations was staged at Camp Phillips, Kansas, under the direction of Lt. Col. Roland F. Charles, MC, who served as the division surgeon for more than two years.

However, even after arriving in England, the training program was far from completed. Additional schooling in the art of saving human life and mock landings on the shores of the English shore line were conducted for the big test to come.

On June 17, 1944, the long-awaited moment neared. D-Day and H-Hour for the division was rapidly approaching. The battalion assembled and the medics moved to their respective units. Each man knew his duty. The crucial test of the medical service was at hand.

During the actual landings on Normandy, casualties were heavy, but the medics' pre-battle training demonstrated its worth and they functioned smoothly. From company aid men to litter bearers to battalion aid stations, then by ambulance to the collecting stations went the sick and wounded, each receiving the finest attention and treatment that modern medical science could offer.

Shortly after the invasion started it was learned under battle conditions that certain changes had to be made. It was found that litter bearers of the regimental medical detachments were expected to perform more gruelling and arduous tasks than they could properly handle. The problem was solved by having the collecting company ambulances haul patients directly from the battalion aid station to the collecting station, thus relieving the collecting company litter bearers of making hauls from the battalion aid station to collecting Points. This method left the company personnel free to be employed as reinforcements for the medical detachment litter bearers. The rolling terrain of western Europe was favorable to this system of ambulance evacuation.

The winter months found the medics in Alsace, and here their duties increased. Pneumonia, trench foot and other winter diseases created additional problems. Evacuation was necessary for the more critical cases. The increase in the number of patients kept the medical teams on the job twenty-four hours a day, seven days a week.

With the beginning of spring, trench foot and pneumonia decreased. But, with the Cross of Lorraine at the banks of the Rhine, extensive and complex plans to handle any situation which might occur had to be mapped out.

Under the arranged plans, one half of the battalion aid station personnel and equipment was to cross the river with the second wave of infantry. On the far shore, a temporary aid station was to be established until such time as the doughboys could move forward. These operations functioned smoothly during the assault of the Rhine beaches. Forward-aid stations were set up several hundred yards behind the advancing troops. Casualties from these stations were immediately sent back to the rear for additional treatment.

At times, the supply situation threatened and became critical, but the well-organized supply system kept the all-important items moving to the front. This smooth system may be credited to the plans made in England, at which time all units were brought up to T/E, Table of Equipment) allowances. During combat, however, each collecting company was furnished with additional expendable supplies enabling them to serve as advance medical equipment dumps. Equipment and supplies then needed by forward groups, such as the 304th, were supplied through the ambulance shuttle system.

With the end of hostilities against Germany, on May 8, 1945, the medical journal revealed that 931 members of the battalion had received awards and decorations in recognition of their outstanding contribution to victory against the enemy. Listed among these outstanding awards were the presentation of thirty-seven Silver Stars, one Cluster to the Silver Star, sixty-two Bronze Stars, three Clusters to the Bronze Star, 506 Purple Hearts for wounds sustained during battle, forty-three Clusters to the Purple Heart, and 279 Combat Medical Badges.

Even with the end of the war in the European Theater of Operations, the work of the combat medic was not finished. Medical supervision was necessary for the civilian population. Thousands of displaced persons urgently needed medical attention. The 79th occupation area was flooded with former slave workers who needed clothing and treatment. Medical and sanitary problems that immediately arose were dealt with decisively. Hospitalization and medical care were provided for the seriously ill. Existing hospital plants were utilized, supplemented by supplies requisitioned through military government channels and captured stocks supplied through regular medical channels.

When the 79th Division moved into the area formerly occupied by the 99th Division, similar problems concerning displaced persons were encountered and solved. In this area the division had charge of nine displaced persons camps with a total population of approximately 44,000 persons. Dispensaries were setup in the camps and five hospitals were established and staffed by foreign medical personnel.

But the work did not end even there. General supervision of the medical and sanitary aspects of the German prisoner of war camps in the division area also fell into the lap of the 304th Battalion. Preventative action against typhus, smallpox, typhoid, and other diseases had to be taken. The work went on without a let-up.

Lt. Col. Tillman D. Johnson, commanding officer of the 304th Medical Battalion, replaced Lt. Col. Roland V. Charles, the division surgeon, on March 9th, and Major Fred D. Lage, became the new battalion commanding officer.

F or the courageous devotion to duty during World War II, the men of the 79th Division hold the medical detachment in high regard. Their record will long live in the hearts of men who fought beside them in this great war.

MINES, BRIDGES, ROADS—
THE KEYNOTE OF THE COMBAT ENGINEERS!

"15 June 1944. Crossed English Channel on Liberty Ship 'John Steele.' Anchored off coast of France, 2100 hours. German planes bombed Utah Beach!"

With that terse note the unit history of the 304th Engineer Combat Battalion in the ETO began. Lieutenant Colonel William G. Van Allen, the outfit's commanding officer, well remembers how maintaining roads, sweeping for mines, and filling craters started before the battalion had time to catch its breath after debarking on the beach. By June 9th, the first bridge built by the unit in a combat area—a timber trestle over the River Gloire—was finished.

The men of the battalion climbed Fort de Roule with the doughboys when they took Cherbourg, and had a finger in just about every phase of that operation. Company A filled in an anti-tank ditch that was holding up tanks and infantry. Company B assisted in the placing of explosives in air vents of the fort, a practice the Germans found most irritating. While fighting still raged in the city, Company C opened the main road into Cherbourg, clearing out several snipers en route.

The Engineers were with forward assault units on the drive into La Haye de Puits and at Bloody Hill, and they stayed that way in the hectic days of rat-racing that marked the division's rapid dash across France. Engineer reconnaissance was in Laval with the first wave, checking potential bridge sites across the Meyenne River. B Company, at the same time, was holding hurried "classes" in a rear area, studying a type of equipment they had never used before—the treadway bridge.

Equipment was moved up immediately upon receipt of the reconnaissance report. Four hours after construction started, vehicles were crossing. That was the record time for the battalion's first treadway!

The role of the battalion in combat continued without pause. At the Seine River Crossing, men and vehicles were moved through a black night and Luftwaffe-infested day with no loss of lives. At the Somme River, working against time, they built three bridges, one with largely on-the-spot material, on a while-you-wait basis for two division spearhead columns and supporting tanks. In the Foret de Parroy, the troops moved on roads the engineers had constructed under fire. In Alsace, the battalion built 59 bridges, laid mines and booby-traps by the thousands—and, when ordered to withdraw, demolished almost 100 bridges, among them many that had been laboriously constructed during the advance. The Rhine was where the battalion supplied one company each to two regiments, an engineer platoon to each assault battalion, and supervised the sweeping, clearing and marking of exit lanes from the far shore for assault units.

In the Foret de Parroy, the 304th Engineers went, in for a chore usually reserved for corps and army engineers: road building. Under constant fire, they hauled sand and gravel— a thousand truckloads of the latter in five days. They laid hundreds of yards of corduroy and Sumervel track. And, when they had finished, the infantry found itself moving through the shell-scarred forest on a military road of surprisingly good quality.

Throughout the operation, the enemy was uncomfortably close. One engineer company had to stop work one day to gather in twelve PWs who had sneaked in through the exposed left flank of one of the regiments.

With combat over, the Engineers still continued their missions. In the Ruhr, they did military government work; while in Czechoslovakia, they helped repair railroads and built a trestle bridge at Eger; and during their stay in Bavaria, winterized numerous displaced persons camps.[201]

---

[201] 79th Division History 148

MEN OF COMPANY A 304TH
COMBAT ENGINEERS BATTALION

NOTE: This list is not complete. These are names we came up with after a 60-year time span.

1) _____ Actkell

2) Willard J. Adams

3) Kilian Albert

4) Anselmo Anaya

5) _____ (Gene) Autry

6) Joseph Bania

7) Clarence J. Barnes

8) Lewis Barnes

9) Cecil Beach

10) Willard K. Beach

11) Andrew A. Benson

12) John A Bercland

13) Robert Brandon

14) Ray Bricher

15) Walter Bucklee

16) David Cameron

17) (Bolo) Capella

18) Jack Carr

19) Lorne Carr

20) Ralph P. Cauble

21) Louis Cavalline

22) Warren Chambelin

23) Eddie J. Champagne (1st Lt.)

24) Myron Christopher

25) P.L. Collins

26) Edward Cooney

27) Dr. Crump

28) Robert Cullen

29) Hugh Cummings

30) Joseph Denchy

31) Jesus C. Diaz

32) Robert Dunham

33) Edmund Ehlmann

34) Ernest Eppler

35) Joe Evaneski

36) Joseph Evans

37) Jesse B. Fairchild

38) Anthony Farace

39) John Fell

40) Jim Floyd

41) Richard E. Frank

42) Lorenso V. Garcia

43) Uree Garner

44) Verl Goforth

45) Ray Gradishor

46) Dallas Gregory

47) Audley P. Guillory

48) Roy Gutherie

49) Alfred A. Haikaara

50) Philip B. Halter

51) Charles R. Hamilton

52) Harlan D. Hansen

53) Charles B. Haradon

54) Robert J. Hardart (Lt.)

55) Ivan Hardyman

56) Emmett Harrison

57) Arthur Hayes Jr.

58) Sidney Hendrix

59) Berg Hilf

60) Thomas Holland

61) Stephen Horan

62) _____ Humphrey

63) Percell Hunt *

64) Willie Hunter

65) George M. Inabinet

66) Glen E. Jacobson (S/Sgt.) *

67) Edgar A. Jarvis

68) James J. Johnson

69) _____ Kaplan (Lt.)

70) Henry C. Kionley

71) William Klimek (Lt.)

72) James Kramer

73) Philip A. Langehough

74) Horace Langston

75) Stanley Laskoski

76) Charles Lemaster

77) William C. Lindsey

78) Eugene Linker

79) Robert McDonald

80) Joseph Macrino (Lt.)

81) _____ Mantilla

82) Paul Marsh

83) Ken McIntosh (S/Sgt.)

84) Robert McComsay

85) James McQuary

86) Earl Mitchell

87) Chester Morgan

88) Verne Motter (Sgt.)

89) Elton MtCastle

90) Joseph Mulato

91) Willis C. Nale

92) Jesse C. Nelson

93) Alex Nemeth

94) William Odom

95) F. Mitchell Oldham

96) Robert F. Opie

97) Maurice Ostepac

98) Robert W. Otto

99) Virgel Pace

100) Kenneth Phelps

101) Bolvar Pokoy *

102) Lionel Potter *

103) John B. Powers *

104) William J. Powers

105) Michael Repucci

106) Arthur Reher

107) William H. Reopell

108) Floryan J. Rolek

109) Andrew Romero

110) Clarence Rose

111) Donald Rudy

112) Anthony Rylka

113) Robert Salazer

114) Marvin C. Sartorius

115) Chad L. Sawyer

116) Cecil Self

117) _____ Shackelford

118) William Sheets

119) Merle L. Smith

120) Ray G. Smith (Lt.)

121) George Stoval

122) Gil Tafel

123) Thomas J. Turrito

124) Rudy G. Thell

125) William Tyre

126) Richard P. Varum (Capt.) *

127) Lewis K. Walter

128) John Warga (Lt.)

129) Albert Webe

130) James Wise

131) William Zilliot

WORKS CITED

Ambrose, Stephen E. *Citizen Soldiers*. New York, New York: Simon & Schuster, 1997.

—D-Day. New York, New York: Simon & Schuster, 1994.

Blumenson, Martin. United States Army in World War II: European Theater of Operations. Breakout and Pursuit Washington DC: Government Printing Office, 1989.

Blunt, Roscoe C. Jr. *Foot Soldier.* New York: Shapedon, 2001.

Bonn, Keith. *When the Odds were Even.* Novato, CA: Presidio Press, 1994.

Boyne, Walter J. *Clash of Wings.* New York, New York: Simon & Schuster, 1994.

Bradley, Omar N. *A General's Life.* New York, New York: Simon & Schuster, 1983.

Carafano, James Jay. *After D-Day:* Operation Cobra and the Normandy Breakout. Boulder, CO: Lynne Rienner Publishing, 2000.

Clarke, Jeffrey and Robert Ross Smith. United States Army in World War II: European Theater of Operations Riviera to the Rhine. Washington, DC: Government Printing Office, 1993.

Collins, Larry & Dominique LaPierre. *Is Paris Burning?* Edison, NJ: Castle Books, 1965.

Conley, Robert, ed. *No End Save Victory.* New York: GP Putnam & Sons, 2001.

Correll, Barett. *Hitler's Generals.* New York: Grove Weidenfeld, 1989.

The Cross of Lorraine: *A Combat History of the 79th Infantry.* Baton Rouge, LA: Army and Navy Publishing Co. 1946.

D'Este, Carlo. Patton: *A Genius for War.* New York: HarpersCollins, 1995.

— *Decision in Normandy.* William S. Konecky Assoc., 2000.

DuPuy, Trevor. *Hitler's Last Gamble.* New York: HarpersCollins, 1994.

Fraser, David. *Knight's Cross.* New York: HarpersCollins, 1993.

Fussell, Paul. Wartime: Understanding Behavior in the Second World War. New York, New York: Oxford University Press, 1989.

Gray, Ed. *General of the Army:* George C. Marshall—Soldier & Statesman. New York, New York: W. W. Norton & Co., 1994.

Hansen, War Diary 8 June 1944

Hastings, Max. *Overlord : D-Day and the battle for Normandy.* New York : Simon and Schuster, 1984.

Hirshon, Stanley P. General *Patton: A Soldier's Life.* New York: HarpersCollins, 2002.

History of the 313th Infantry in World War II. Washington, DC: Infantry Journal Press, 1947.

Hogg, Ian. *Twentieth Century Artillery.* New York: Barnes and Noble, 2000.

Keegan, John. *Six Armies in Normandy.* Viking Press, 1982.

—. *Churchill's Generals.* New York: Grove Weidenfeld, 1991.

Kennedy, David M. *Freedom from Fear.* New York: Oxford University Press, 1999.

Kindsvatter, Peter S. *American Soldiers.* Lawrence, KS: University Press, 2003.

Larrabee, Eric. *Commander in Chief: Franklin Delano Roosevelt, His Lieutenants, and Their War.* Harper and Row, 1989.

Leckie, Robert. *Helmet for My Pillow.* New York: Doubleday, 1979

Lewin, Ronald. *Ultra Goes to War.* New York: McGraw-Hill, 1978.

Martin, Ralph G. *The GI War, 1941-1945.* Boston: Little, Brown, 1967.

May, Ernest R. *Strange Victory—Hitler's Conquest of France.* Hill & Wang: New York, 2000.

Megaree, Geoffrey P. *Inside Hitler's Command.* University Press of Kansas, 2000.

Overy, Richard. *Why the Allies Won.* New York: W. W. Norton, 1995.

Pogue, Forrest C. *George C. Marshall: Ordeal and Hope:* Vol. 2. New York: Viking Press, 1964.

—. George C. Marshall: *Organizer of Victory,* Vol. 3. New York: Viking Press, 1973.

Province, Charles M. *Patton's Third Army.* New York: Hippocrene Books, 1992.

Pyle, Ernie. *Here is Your War: The Story of GI Joe.* Nebraska: University of Nebraska Press, 2004.

—. *Brave Men.* Nebraska: University of Nebraska Press, 2002.

Rosner, Bernat, and Frederic C. Tubach, with Sally Patterson Tubach. *An Uncommon Friendship: From Opposite Sides of the Holocaust.* Berkeley: Univ. of California Press, 2001

Sereny, Gitta. *Albert Speer—His Battle with Truth.* New York: Albert Knopf, 1995.

Shirer, William L. *20th Century Journey Volume II: The Nightmare Years.* Boston: Little, Brown & Co., 1984.

Strawson, John. *Hitler as Military Commander.* New York, NY: Barnes and Noble, 1971.

Von Luck, Hans. *Panzer Commander.* New York, NY: Dew 1989

Weigley, Russell. *Eisenhower's Lieutenants.* Bloomington, IN: Indiana University Press, 1990.

Whiting, Charles. *America's Forgotten Army.* Rockville Centre, NY: Sarpedon, 1999

Wilder, Amos N. *"Armageddon Revisited: a World War I Journal."* New Haven : Yale University Press, 1994.

Williamson, Murray. *Luftwaffe.* Baltimore MD: The Nautical Aviation Company, 1985.

Williamson, Murray and Allen R. Millett. *A War to be Won: Fighting the Second World War.* Cambridge MA: Belknap Press, 2000.

Willis, Donald J. *The Incredible Year.* Iowa: Iowa State Press, 1988.

Winters, Harold A. *Battling the Elements.* Baltimore: Johns Hopkins Press, 1998.

World War II Magazine
James L. Thompson, p.8
"Quest for the Eternal City" Eric Niderost, July 2003. pp 38-44
David T. Zabecki - *Odyssey of a Landser* WWII magazine Sept 2003 p. 56

Zoepf, Wolfe T. *Seven Days in January.* Bedford, PA: The Aberjona Press, 2001.